Love Bade Me Welcome

Love Bade Me Welcome

ROBERT LLEWELYN

Paulist Press
New York/Mahwah

This book was first published in 1984 by Darton, Longman & Todd Ltd, London.

Author's royalties earned by the sale of the American edition of this book are being given to the Order of Julian of Norwich in Norwich, Connecticut.

Library of Congress
Catalog Card Number: 85–60417

ISBN: 0–8091–2715–6

Published by Paulist Press
997 Macarthur Boulevard
Mahwah, New Jersey 07430

Printed and bound in the
United States of America

Contents

Acknowledgements

The calligraphy of the poem 'Love Bade Me Welcome' by George Herbert is copyright © Elizabeth Griffiths and reproduced opposite with her permission.

Thanks are also due to William Collins, Sons & Co. Ltd for permission to quote from *The Mirror Mind* by William Johnston, SJ.

Love bade me welcome:
yet my soul drew back.
                guilty of dust and sin.
But quick-eyed Love,
observing me grow slack.
            from my first entrance in.
Drew nearer to me.
sweetly questioning,
            if I lacked anything.

"A guest," I answered.
"Worthy to be here,"
        Love said You shall be he".
"I, the unkind, ungrateful?
ah my dear, I cannot
                    look on thee".
Love took my hand,
and smiling did reply.
        "Who made the eyes but I?"

Truth Lord, but I have marred
them; let my shame go
            where it doth deserve."
"And know you not," says Love,
"Who bore the blame?"
        "My dear then I will serve."
"You must sit down," says Love,
"And taste my meat."
                so I did sit and eat.

George Herbert

Preface

This book takes its origin from a series of Lent lectures given this year in Norwich Cathedral under the title 'Prayer: God's Love and Man's Response'. They have, however, been largely re-written and expanded and in effect four of the chapters are entirely new.

Basically, the subject of the book is the life of prayer. But prayer becomes true only as the distortions affecting our image of God are corrected. Hence the first section is given to examining what we believe about God with a view to correcting our vision where it may prove to be inadequate or wrong. Only then are we ready to speak authentically of the prayer life to which the second section is devoted.

The first three chapters are an expansion of a single lecture and are aimed at developing the teaching of Julian of Norwich that there is no wrath in God. The book was completed before the recent events at York Minster brought the subject prominently before the public. Various explanations have been offered for the lightning flash which brought destruction, not a few attributing it to the direct expression of God's anger evoked by an ecclesiastical decision with which they (and in the first place, God) disagreed. Others, not surprisingly, have protested that such a view is altogether too simplistic and naive; and, moreover, it is abhorrent to their understanding of the character of God.[1] Yet no one, so far as I am aware, has raised voice to question the merits of a theology which in the first place affirms a God in whom wrath may be found. Julian will not allow such a conception; her teaching is that the wrath – which she describes as a perversity and opposition to peace and love – is in us and not in God. Here is a message full of hope yet allowing no false confidence in presuming upon God's goodness. It is full of hope because it means that God in whom no wrath can exist is always actively willing to heal the corruption within us, to draw us into closer union with himself, in whatever state we may now be. It allows no false confidence because in wilfully resisting God I am by the operation of an internal spiritual law turning his unadulterated love into 'wrath', though that wrath is not in him but in me. The rain falls ever clear and pure from the heavens but that which alights on poisoned vegetation itself takes on the nature of poison, yet the corruption was not in the rain but in the ground on which it fell. If you still choose to call it God's rain I must at once reply that it is not the rain as it came from God. And the rain, clean and fresh, continues to fall, however poisoned the land may be. The illustration breaks down at this point. The poisoned land is the corrupt heart, which may be open to receive God's goodness which then becomes a cleansing and renewing agent; or it may close itself, deliberately rejecting the same goodness, which, so long as this attitude persists, works towards a deeper wrath or corruption within. Whichever way it may be, the unchanging compassionate love of God as it meets every man and woman remains constant; the variable factor belongs to a later stage.

Having myself – through Julian – come to this view, I cannot but wish to share it with others who may be helped as I have been. Julian's teaching is not simply a theological nicety; it makes a tremendous difference, as I have tried to show, to our attitude both to ourselves and others if we accept it as true. Julian proclaimed her truth six hundred years ago at a time when God was presented widely as a harsh and forbidding figure who would at the last exercise vengeance and retribution on those who had failed to meet his stern demands. It was a bold and courageous pronouncement to make in those far-off days and it is scarcely surprising that the message of an obscure and 'unlettered' woman passed largely unheeded. After centuries of near oblivion Julian is undoubtedly being rediscovered today because the climate is right to receive her. There are strong indications that this is so, as I have pointed out in the text, in the forms of worship drawn up in the Alternative Service Book of 1980 from which all references to the wrath of God found in the Book of Common Prayer have been excluded. It is, of course, true that the ASB does not cancel the familiar usage of 1662, but one can hardly be wrong in attaching strong significance to the omissions to which I have referred.

It must be borne in mind that Julian wrote throughout for the encouragement of her 'even-Christians', people like ourselves,

who long to know and love God better, but who through the
frailty of our nature and the weakness of our wills fall frequently,
and need to be rescued not once but many times by the compassionate love which is ever at hand to raise us up. Unlike some of
the saints Julian had no 'ladder' to be mounted rung by rung until
we are at last poised to step off into the heavenly places. Her
picture is, rather, of children learning to walk, who frequently fall
flat on their faces and need to be helped back on to their feet
once more to make again their halting steps to the place where
they would be. It is, too, for such people – you and me – that the
present book is intended. Julian would have us see that 'whether
we be clean or foul' there is no such thing as an angry God
standing over against us – always the fountain pours forth water
pure and clear – but, rather, that the compassionate love of God
is acting at all times to abate and dispel what she calls the 'wrath'
within ourselves.

Our book takes its title from George Herbert's widely known
poem which is printed before this Preface. It is a poem of deep
tenderness and beauty and the reader may sometimes like to pick
up this book for the sake of it alone. Life is deeper than logic and
poetry may take us to its heart more surely than the more exacting
medium of prose. I would like to draw attention especially to the
surprise twist which the poem takes in its last few lines. We are
there reminded how our first impulse on accepting Love's welcome
is to look about for some form of service. Yet there follows at
once a gentle rebuke. May it not be that Love wants to serve us,
and, if so, are we too proud to submit? 'You must sit down,' says
Love, 'and taste my meat.' It is this which engages our intention
in the second half of the book. Here is no escape from the realities
of life but, rather, to those who are called, an entrance at its
deepest level. It is only as our love takes on the nature of God's
own love that we can offer to one another the nourishment which
alone can satisfy. And while our love must be mainly expressed
in daily living, its roots are discoverable in the depths of the prayer
life. The feeding at God's table precedes the command to go out
in peace to love and serve the world.

I have not followed Julian in the final chapters on prayer. Julian
gives us the theological background from which prayer must be
made. She offers encouragement in our prayers and warns us
against slackness when the going is hard. But nowhere does she
tell us how to go about the actual business of praying. After an

introductory chapter establishing principles behind the prayer life which are to be kept in mind throughout, of which the most important is that only the Holy Spirit can be our teacher, I have outlined very simply some well-tried methods of prayer. All of these have been a support to me at one time or another and this book is little more than an attempt to share with the reader what I have found helpful. This includes the brief examination of *one* way of Zen practice, mostly relegated to the Appendix, so that only those who have a special interest need pursue it. It is a great advance that we live in a time in which openness to what is good in other traditions has been encouraged at the highest level by both the Roman Catholic and the Anglican Church.

In one major respect I have departed from the pattern of the Cathedral lectures. In those I made *The Cloud of Unknowing* the foundation for our understanding of contemplative prayer. Having written several books[2] in which *The Cloud* is prominent, I would have found it impossible to have made the same approach here without wearisome repetition. I have, therefore, touched only very briefly on *The Cloud*, leaving readers to pursue the subject elsewhere if they wish.

August 1984

Robert Llewelyn,
The Julian Shrine,
c/o All Hallows,
Rouen Road,
Norwich

Notes

1 The reality of signs in themselves is not in question. The resurrection, on which the York controversy was centred, was itself a sign (Matthew 12:39–40) – the Church proclaims it as the greatest of all signs. In view of the varied declarations of faith evoked by the debate I would like to affirm not only my own belief in the bodily resurrection of Jesus but, further, my conviction that in its denial something of considerable theological importance is lost. For the event points not simply to itself but beyond itself to matters of cosmic significance. As Bishop Gore wrote more than half a century ago: 'The Church has always claimed for the resurrection that it possesses not only religious but metaphysical value, as throwing light not merely on the destiny of men, but also on the destiny of the material universe, and its relation to spirit.' Our

present conception of matter as a form of energy may well make this belief more understandable to us than it could have been to our ancestors.

2 *Prayer and Contemplation* (SLG Press, Fairacres, Oxford 1975). I have in a few places drawn on the text of this book and express my gratitude to the SLG Press; *With Pity not with Blame* (Darton Longman and Todd 1982); *The Dart of Longing Love* (Darton Longman and Todd 1983). *Cloud* references in the present book have been taken from this source.

Part One

God's Love

1

Love Bade Me Welcome

'Jane, darling, what are you doing?'

A mother glanced eagerly down to the floor where her six-year-old daughter lay engrossed in some complicated work of art.

'Why, Mummy, I'm drawing God.'

'But, darling, nobody knows what God looks like.'

'No, Mummy, they don't know yet, but they will when they've seen my drawing.'

This, too, is my hope, the difference being that whereas Jane's picture was original, my own, I am convinced, is embedded in – though by no means always extracted from – the heart of the New Testament.

Young and old, we all have our picture of God. Many factors have gone into its composition. Chief among these, perhaps, for most readers of this book, is the influence of the Church. For some it will be through the Church's teaching and worship; for others, less obviously, through culture and environment, through the attitudes and influences surrounding us when we were children.

There are many places in the Bible to which we might turn in our quest for the vision of God. The vision of God means the vision of Love. We shall begin our search by considering again the familiar and well-loved story of the prodigal son.[1]

A man has two sons. The younger asked his father for the share of the estate that would one day come to him. So the father divided the property between them. A few days later the younger son gathered together everything he had, and left for a distant country where he squandered his money in a life of debauchery.

We know the rest of the story: the famine, the hunger, the squalor, the loneliness, the young man coming eventually to his senses and taking the resolution to make the homeward trek, if perchance his father might receive him. We recall too the reaction of the elder brother and that too will have point in what we shall say. The parable is in fact much more aptly named as that of the two sons.

We join the story as the younger son draws near to his father's house. What we must now note is that everything that happens to this young man exceeds his wildest expectations.

Uppermost in his mind is the hope that his father will receive him. Doubtless he knows his father well enough to believe that that will be so. It may be a rather solemn affair, a well-deserved rebuke, perhaps, a reminder of the suffering and anxiety he has caused his loving parents; but ending, no doubt, in forgiveness and in life once again in the security of the farm, if only as a paid servant.

But what happens? We read that when he was still a long way off his father saw him, was moved with compassion and ran to meet him, taking him into his arms and kissing him tenderly.

And more. He hoped, no doubt, that clean and serviceable clothing might be given him to replace his worn and tattered garments. Yet what does he hear? 'Bring quickly the best robe, and put it on him; and put a ring on his hand, and shoes on his feet.'

Yet more again. He is hungry and exhausted and longs for a square meal to sustain him. Never had he dreamt that his father would call for the fatted calf to be killed and a feast held in his honour.

And yet the best is still to come. It had been his plan to ask his father to take him back as a farm hand. His heart thrills as he learns that his sonship has never lapsed. 'This my son was dead, and is alive again; he was lost, and is found.'

In this picture of a good and loving father Jesus has given us an insight into the character of God.

We are all prodigals – at least God grant that it may be so, for the alternative is to bear the proud and self-righteous image of the elder son. And we are prodigals not just once, in some sudden and dramatic sowing of our wild oats (in the lives of most of us there may indeed be no event of that sort), but in that we stray frequently day by day and as often need to make our way back into the outstretched arms of God. But sometimes it seems to us – after a particularly grievous fall, perhaps – that the face of God is set against us, and it may be we are fearful lest we cannot be received. We learn from this parable not only that the heart of God is always open to receive us, but that the manner of our reception exceeds in generosity and compassion anything we are likely in our wildest hopes to imagine.

Although the Bible story tells us much about the father's generosity to the returning son, it says nothing of the father's feelings towards him while he was still in his sins. Can we fill in the picture at this point?

A village preacher in India – a Christian from the depressed classes, who at one time were called the outcastes – a man poor in knowledge but rich in wisdom, used to tell the story of the prodigal son to the Hindus of the surrounding villages. He was not afraid to embellish it and he would tell his hearers how every night the father, before he went to bed, would hang a lighted lantern in the porch and say to his wife: 'Who knows but our boy may return tonight? I would not like there to be no light to welcome him.' The preacher's bishop said that this was inspired comment.

How then are we to describe the father's emotions in the absence of his son? Grief? That would be a suitable word. Compassion? That, too, would ring true. A deep yearning for the boy's return? We can hardly be wrong there. Sorrow and sadness born of deep abhorrence for the harm he was doing to himself and others? It would seem that we are still on safe grounds. But anger? – no. The story would not for a moment support that. The village preacher had it right. At every stage the father's love is marked by deep tenderness and compassion, and not only towards this boy but towards the elder son with whom he reasoned so patiently. If any doubt remains, consider another story from the same chapter in St Luke's Gospel: the shepherd in search of the sheep which has strayed. Care, concern, love, tenderness, all these things. But anger – no.[2]

The point needs emphasis because it frequently eludes us. We know quite well that when we repent and turn again to God for acceptance and forgiveness we are met by the graciousness and goodness of God. We may know much less well that when we are still in our sins, the graciousness and compassion of God is following us there too, and we do not have to look for any change on God's part when we return; the change is in us and not in him. God's face is never turned towards us in anger even when we are in our sins.

Now that is a very bold thing to say. I would go further and say that it is for many Christians a revolutionary thing to say.

Leave aside for the time being the many passages in the Bible where we hear of God's wrath thundering upon the heathen or the children of disobedience – those who reject him and flout his laws – and bring the matter within the sphere of the Church, the toiling, striving, yearning people of God whose hope it is through prayer and the regular feeding upon word and sacrament, to walk faithfully in what God would have them do.

If we examine the Book of Common Prayer on which the Christian life of almost all Anglican readers has been formed, we shall not find, it is true, many allusions to God's wrath, but such as there are indicate that the Reformers held an image of God to which very few instructed Christians would be likely to conform today.

Taking the book in chronological order, we find an optional introductory sentence to matins and evensong which asks that we may be spared God's anger but not his judgement. This verse from Jeremiah yields an important theological truth. It does, of course, assume the possibility of God's wrath but it makes the point that judgement – and judgement may be adverse – is not necessarily to be linked with anger. Later, in the course of matins, we have as the only set canticle at that point a psalm which presents a God who in an outburst of irrational rage banishes for ever a disobedient people from his sight. In every Eucharist we are bidden to acknowledge God's wrath and indignation against us. The Litany allows for the possibility of God's anger resting on the praying Church for ever. In the baptismal service, prayer is made that infants may be delivered from God's wrath; and reference to his anger appears again in the visitation of the sick. Finally, in the commination service (admittedly seldom used today, though some will remember it) we have reference not only to God's wrath but to his vengeance as well, and the possibility of God raining down 'fire and brimstone' upon sinners is vividly portrayed.

In liturgy, theology is taught largely by unconscious absorption. Words matter, they stand for us as symbols, and although we may not stop to think about them and analyse them, the concepts for which they stand sink deeply into the unconscious mind and affect our behaviour and response in ways of which we may not be aware. Psychology has made us more conscious of this today than in former times, and whatever shortcomings we may find in our new forms of worship, reference to God's wrath and indignation and the like have been corrected,[3] and we offer our worship more closely to God as he truly is. This is of the utmost importance for the authenticity of our prayer life.

But there have, too, been voices in the past who would offer a strong and fervent Amen to what I am saying. One such person is Julian of Norwich. In her revelations it was shown her that there was no anger in God. God, she said, was that goodness which cannot be angry, for God is nothing but goodness.[4] Or again, 'that it is against the property of [God's] power to be angry, and against the property of his wisdom, and against the property of his goodness'. And this, she insists, is true at all times, not just in the times of faithfulness and response, but no less when we fall away and our lives are marked by weakness, failure, and forgetfulness of God.

What is our reaction to words such as these? A sometime professor at a theological school in the United States has written that Julian's spirituality is sentimental and soft-minded, that it is not for clear and dynamic thinkers. During my lifetime a number of saints and writers of a past age have enjoyed popularity. When I was young it was Thomas à Kempis, then came Francis of Assisi, and a little later Francis de Sales, with a lesser interest in Fénelon and de Caussade. Since then St John-of-the-Cross and St Teresa have enjoyed increasing popularity. Now Julian of Norwich is coming to the fore and I make bold to say she will hold the field within the next twenty years. A dynamic thinker such as the late Bishop John Robinson has described her theology as 'astonishingly whole and extraordinarily modern'[5] and Thomas Merton has considered her one of the two greatest English theologians of all time. Richard Harries, Dean of King's College, has in a radio talk ventured the opinion that she may prove to be the greatest woman England has produced.

It is certainly true that an increasing number of people are discovering Julian today and look to her not simply as a mystical and devotional writer who brings them comfort and strength, but, too, as no mean theologian, who has important things to say. The true theologian is one whose vision of God is authentic or true. It is on target; he or she sees God as he is. We all have our vision of God but in some degree, we know, it misses the mark, and we worship to some extent the God who isn't rather than the God who is. On this point of anger in God, or, more accurately, on the absence of anger in God, Julian, I believe, corrects the vision many Christians have upheld. And as we have noted, in this

matter of wrath the Church of our day, through the Alternative
Service Book (ASB) of 1980, appears, if not to endorse, at least
to be moving in the direction of Julian's theology.

But, to return to Julian, we must note that although she says
that there can be no anger in God, she does not exclude the idea
of anger altogether. There is indeed wrath, and plenty of it, but
it is, she says, not in God but in us. This she describes as 'a
perversity and opposition to peace and love'. If Julian were writing
in the idiom of today I think she would say that we project our
own anger on to God and then see it wrongly as God's anger
directed towards us. We are probably familiar enough with this
process in our relationships with one another. We think so-and-
so is angry and ill disposed towards us and then realize later that
it is we who were angry, projecting our own anger on to this other
person, and seeing it there we mistake it for their anger and not
our own. In the same sort of way it may often seem to us that we
are the object of God's wrath, but it is not really so. Julian gives
expression to this thought in the following passage from chapter
40 of her *Revelations of Divine Love*:

> And this is a supreme friendship of our courteous Lord, that
> he protects us so tenderly while we are in our sins, and shows
> us our sins by the sweet light of mercy and grace. But when we
> see ourselves so foul then we believe that God may be angry
> with us because of our sins. Then we are moved by the Holy
> Spirit through contrition to prayer and we desire with all our
> heart an amendment of ourselves to appease God's anger until
> the time that we can find rest of soul and ease of conscience.
> And then we hope that God has forgiven us our sin and this is
> true. And our courteous Lord shows himself to the soul,
> welcoming it as a friend as if it had been in pain and in prison
> saying, 'My dear darling, I am glad you have come to me in all
> your woe. I have always been with you and now you see me
> loving and we are made one in bliss.'

Julian is here saying that in the time of our sinning we *believe*
God to be angry with us and that this knowledge (as we believe
it to be), through the action of the Holy Spirit, acts as a spur to
repentance and amendment of life until such time as we find
peace. Our vision (she says) is in fact false; our sinful state (the
wrath in us) has blinded us. God has not in fact at any stage been
angry (in the sense of annoyance, antagonism, much less fury or

rage), but has throughout been watching over us in tenderness and compassion and drawing us with his love. But this we *see* to be the case only after we have been 'made one in bliss'.

There are, however, some for whom it is abhorrent to believe that God is never angry; God's anger 'when deserved' is evidence of his love, a reassurance that he cares. As it is commonly expressed, God's anger and his love are but two sides of one coin. Moreover, they will say, that when they sin they need the knowledge of God's anger as a stimulus to help them to turn to him again. If it could ever be proved to them that God could never be angry, then the incitement to repentance would be lost and they themselves in mortal danger. It would not generally be wise to try to persuade such people otherwise. The stage may be assumed to be a necessary one and the Holy Spirit should be left to do his deepening work in his own time. Their experience is that which Julian describes, except that they have not received as yet final revelation of which the passage speaks.

There may well be occasions when anger may act as a spur to the will, and St Paul's well-known injunction has application here.[6] But it will not always be so. Anger or the fear of anger can paralyse the will, and a sensitive person and especially a child may be discouraged and even driven to despair. That, too, has its counterpart in God's dealings with us though it does not find expression in the passage quoted. What the passage does reveal is that since God is in no situation angry with us, we may in the time of our falling reach out to him in the faith that it is his *compassion* which is even then operative towards us. This is not to be a lighthearted presumption on God's generosity but is the way of reverent fear of which Julian speaks in chapter 74: she says that it is the only form of fear which fully pleases God. At the same time Julian recognizes the way of 'doubtful fear' illustrated in the previous paragraph, seeing this as a stage on the way, 'for it can never please our Lord that his servants doubt in his goodness'.

Julian, then, would have us come to the knowledge that God will in no circumstances be angry with us. He will not because he cannot, and he cannot because there is no wrath in him. Ultimately we are to learn to walk before him in the way of reverent fear, though 'doubtful fear' must first be met and passed through.

What is this reverent fear? Let Julian describe it in her own words:

Reverent fear is that which makes us hastily to flee
  from everything that is not good,
And to fall into our Lord's breast,
  as the child into the mother's arms,
  with all our intention and with all our mind,
  knowing our feebleness and our great need,
  knowing his everlasting goodness and his blessed love,
  seeking only in him for salvation,
  cleaving to him with faithful trust.
That fear which leads us in this direction
  is gentle and gracious and good and true.
And all that is opposed to this is either wrong or mixed
  with wrong . . .
Thus in love we shall be familiar and close to God,
  and in fear we shall be gentle and courteous to God.[7]

Notes

1 Luke 15:11–32.
2 It may be said that we are not justified in pressing the details of a parable in this way. After all, where would we be if we deduced an image of God from the parable of the unjust judge? The point is valid. However, I think it can be said that the parables, while proving nothing about anger in God, point in the direction indicated. But it is enough if they are seen simply as setting the scene and providing the background for the arguments which follow.
3 Since writing this I find – to my surprise – that in the ASB, reference to God's anger is made in an optional prayer in the funeral service. Even more surprisingly, where the Book of Common Prayer speaks merely of God's displeasure, the ASB uses anger. Thus 'art justly displeased' becomes 'are justly angered'. With reference to the ASB passages which exclude wrath, it must be remembered that the Book of Common Prayer is not 'cancelled' by the ASB. Even so, the mind of the revisers seems abundantly clear from the alterations made.
4 *Julian of Norwich. Showings*, ch. 46. Translated by Edmund Colledge, OSA and James Walsh, SJ. SPCK, 'The Western Classics of Spirituality' series 1978. Julian's book is usually known as *The Revelations of Divine Love*. See ch. 45–50 for absence of wrath in God.
5 *The Roots of a Radical* (p. 148) by John A. T. Robinson. SCM Press 1980.
6 Ephesians 4:26–7. 'Be angry but do not sin; do not let the sun go down on your anger, and give no opportunity to the devil' (RSV).

7 *Julian of Norwich. Showings* (see note 4 above), ch. 74. The first four words are slightly adapted.

2

A Question Answered

It is possible that at this stage there will be two questions in the minds of some. It may be said that what has been written is all very well for those who are likely to be reading this book. It may not be true for all, but for most it is probably true to say that it is their desire to serve God and to search out his plan for their lives. Sometimes, we know only too well, we fall away in our weakness, and it is encouragement and understanding and compassion which we need to set us back on the path again. We can be agreed that to speak of the anger of God in this situation would be inappropriate and in any case it would not help.

But what of others who do not believe in God or who, believing, have no care for him? What of the vast majority of men and women whose minds are set on worldly hopes and ambitions? Or what of those who pursue a life of vice and crime? If God is, as Julian insists, that goodness which cannot be angry then here, too, there can be no anger?

Yes, that is so – there can be no anger. We stand on treacherous grounds when we introduce an 'us' and a 'them' into our thinking. If we are considering what radiates unceasingly from the being of God then there are no distinctions among us. God makes his sun to shine on the good and the evil and his rain to fall on the just and the unjust. If, however, we are thinking of the effect of the sunshine and the rain then a further factor is introduced. The sun which ripens one man's fruit may scorch another's pasture. The rain which fills one farmer's pond may beat down another's corn. Yet it is the same sunshine and the same rain for one and all. So, too, translating our rough and ready analogy, God's unadulterated love, free from every tinge of wrath, ever 'leaps forth' from his eternal glory, but its effect upon us depends on whether, on the one hand, we welcome it (or desire to welcome it, praying as Julian's 'even-Christians' that we may be given the grace to do so), or whether, on the other, we deliberately ignore it or wilfully and persistently reject it. This is not to suggest that we can ever tell whether any do, in fact, belong to this latter category, and it must be unprofitable to speculate on such matters. There were those who were last who shall be first, receiving their call only towards the end of the day (Matthew 20:6). At least it must be the hope of every Christian that, ultimately, Love shall be everywhere triumphant.

Julian is not the only writer of earlier times to endorse our thoughts at this point. William Law, best known for his spiritual classic *A Serious Call to a Devout and Holy Life* (1728), was in his later life firmly of the opinion that in no circumstances whatever could there be wrath in God. Law, it is true, does in chapter 10 of his *Serious Call* refer to wrath in God, saying that 'rebels against [God]' are 'subject to his wrath'. However, twenty-four years later, when he wrote what is commonly regarded as his best book, *The Spirit of Love* (1752–4), he goes to great lengths to prove that God can in no circumstances exercise anger, for the completely sufficient reason that this can be no part of his nature. The book is written mostly in the form of a dialogue between three people of whom Theophilus, who is the main speaker, is clearly the mouthpiece of Law. A few quotations must suffice.[1]

> It is much more possible for the sun to give forth darkness than for God to do, or be, or give forth anything but blessedness or goodness (p. 358).
>
> God can no more begin to have any wrath, rage, or anger in Himself after nature and creature are in a fallen state than He could have been infinite wrath and boundless rage everywhere and from all eternity. For nothing can begin to be in God, or in a new state in Him, as the Triune nature of His Deity (p. 392).
>
> For nothing can be in God but that which He is and has from Himself, and therefore no wrath can be in the Deity itself unless God was in Himself before all nature and from all eternity, an infinity of wrath (p. 393).

We may pause to consider the implications of what Law (and Julian before him) is saying. Have you been negligent in prayer and worship? God is not angry with you. Have you neglected to visit some sick person you should have seen? God is not angry with you. Have you committed some deeply shameful and perhaps criminal offence? God is not angry with you. No, no, don't get

me wrong. If you persist in rejecting the goodness of God which
would draw you to himself, only hell can await you – if you are
not already there. But if you are there, God's compassion is
following you, drawing you, calling you, eager to love you back
to himself. He is not angry with you for it is not in his nature to
be angry. No more can a tree bear fruit contrary to its nature
than can God be angry with a living soul. Jesus was not angry
with the good thief on the cross, though doubtless many painful
memories lay behind him. Nor is there anything to suggest that
he was angry with the impenitent thief, even though hell lay
before him. He would have drawn him too with the same cords
of love if the wrath within the man himself had not prevented it.

Some readers may be shocked at what I have written; others
may think my words unnecessarily provocative. They are not
written to encourage any to commit offences from the least to the
greatest. They are written because, if you believe God is angry
with you, you are likely to be driven more deeply into darkness
and despair. It is the goodness of God and not the wrath of God
which draws you to himself. And that goodness is operative even
while you are in your sins. It is not that God is angry with you at
one stage and then later 'repents' and draws you in some other
way. There is a story on those lines in the Old Testament (Exodus
32:7–14) but you would not believe it if you heard it preached
today. You would say that it portrays a conception of God which
you could not take seriously.

I say these things, then, because our belief that God's blame
and anger rests upon us when we have fallen into sin may act as
a heavy weight upon the spirit, hindering our return to him. It is
not so, and until its spell upon us is broken we cannot know the
fullness of peace and joy. All Julian's 'even-Christians' must allow
this truth to burn deeply into their hearts, a truth which she
proclaims repeatedly in her writings: 'When we fall, quickly he
raises us up with his loving embrace and his gracious touch. And
when we are strengthened by his sweet working, then we willingly
choose him by his grace, that we shall be his servants and his
lovers, constantly and for ever.'[2] And again: '*And in the time of
our sinning* [my italics] he shows to us the demeanour of ruth
and pity, mightily protecting us and defending us against all our
enemies.'[3]

It is partly because God (and Jesus too) has been so often seen
as a stern and forbidding judge that the Church has turned in

large measure to the virgin mother, seeing in her qualities which
in truth belong to God.[4] I remember that when I was young I was
once told that Roman Catholics worshipped the virgin Mary, and
I expect I shared my informant's belief that that was a shocking
thing to do. Yet supposing it were true and that some uninstructed
Catholic, in worshipping the virgin Mary, carried over into his
worship a character picture of God as he truly is (though the
worshipper gave him another name and that name was Mary)
then such a man would have been nearer to eternal truth and
goodness than his orthodox Catholic brother who worshipped a
being whom he *called* God, taking over into his worship a conception of the Deity which was seriously warped. If the Indian peasant
who worships OHO[5] could have before him the true mental picture
of the God and Father of our Lord Jesus Christ,[6] he would be
closer to God than the Christian who worships a badly distorted
likeness of him whom he names God. Julian has corrected my
own wrong picture held for many years. So it was that recently,
when approached by a book research association, I was able to
name *The Revelations of Divine Love* as the book which had
influenced me most in my lifetime. Of course, in large measure,
with all my 'even-Christians', my picture still falls short and I have
still to absorb into my being what are as yet the concepts of the
mind. In technical language, what is notional must become fully
experiential. The descent of the mind to the heart, as the desert
fathers put it, must continue to the end. To read a signpost is not
the same thing as to make a journey, though it may well spell the
difference between a journey which is profitable and one which
is not.

What a difference it makes in my relationship to others if I
believe there can be no anger in God! If I meet someone on
whom I believe God's anger may rest, then in so far as my own
life is hidden with Christ in God, my attitude must, it seems, be
some reflection of God's. Thus I shall be in some degree hostile
from the first and our relationship must be impaired. But how can
I ever know that God's anger does not rest in some measure upon
everyone I meet, unless I know that it can rest on no one, since
anger is not possible to God?

I return to the manuscript two months after writing the last
paragraph, to relate an incident which illustrates its point. Early
yesterday evening as I stepped into the church from the Julian cell
I saw a youth at the altar obviously looking round for something to

steal. I had watched him for nearly a minute examining the orna-
ments when he turned and saw me and walked hurriedly from the
church. As he passed I asked if there was anything I could do for
him but, hardly surprisingly, he decided no. Following him into
the alley I called on him to stop which, to my surprise, he immediately did. However, when I reached him he put up his fists in a
boxing stance and stood motionless as if to say 'attack if you dare'.
I told him that I only wanted to help him, but for a full minute
he stood with his fists at the ready. During this time I asked him
what took him to the church to steal and he replied that if you
needed money that was the only way to get it. Replying 'not
quite', I took a pound from my pocket and gave it to him. He
took it with some surprise and said thank you. His fists now being
down he produced a tin of tobacco, rolled himself a cigarette, and
passing the tin to me asked me to help myself. Although I belong
to 'the opposite camp' this was clearly a time when an exchange
of hospitality was indicated. We then got talking. He told me his
name and that he was an unemployed school leaver and he said
a little of his family and broken home. I offered him a further
pound and this he refused until (perhaps unwisely) I pressed it on
him. We parted on good terms and he asked if he could come to
the church and have a further talk, saying that if he came back
he wouldn't steal. And on my part, if he comes, I shall not be
giving him any more money as that, by putting a strain on his
motivation, would hinder rather than help.

What was it which made me behave in this 'foolish' way? It was
nothing but the reflection, reinforced no doubt by the writing of
this book, that since God was not angry with this young man how
senseless would it be for me to be so! Time was when I would
have reacted very differently and, being theologically minded, I
would have seen my 'wrath' as but a human reflection of God's.
It seems that the approach 'worked', as they say, but it might, of
course, have ended otherwise with the loss of my wallet, which,
though hardly a disaster on the cosmic scale, would have given
the opportunity for a good deal of wise-acreing and tut-tutting.
No doubt it will still, though what I did was little enough. 'Love
thy neighbour', said George Herbert, adding shrewdly, for the
limitations of our human nature 'yet pull not down thine hedge.'
I have to confess that that is where I belong; a couple of blossoms
from an ample hedgerow were not much to spare. However, the
point of the story, obviously, lies elsewhere.

Shortly after I had written this, the young man, true to his intention of yesterday, returned to the church for a talk. One hopes that something useful came of it. At any rate, before he left, he smiled for the first time.

While I have been writing this chapter, a priest has come to talk over a tragic event in his parish. Alan, as we shall call him, is a young man of twenty-one now in police custody after battering his eight-week-old son so severely that it looks as if the child will die. Alan and his young wife have for several months been communicant members of the parish church. They say their prayers and read their Bibles as many other Christians do. Alan is in a state of shock, anguish and bewilderment. So, too, is his wife who stands firmly beside him; she was not there when the incident took place. 'John', the parish priest, has been with Alan in the police cell. John, who is clearly himself bearing a great deal of the pain, regards Alan with a deep and loving compassion and is doing what he can to help him make a positive response and to prevent him sinking into the morass of despair. John is not angry with Alan; he could not help him if it were so. And in so far as John is truly a minister of God, it must be that his attitude reflects God's attitude. God, too, bears the pain, the total pain of the situation, the father–mother–child pain, the parish pain, and through the pain would draw Alan to himself. If I do not believe this but believe instead that God is angry, then I have to tell John, who has come to see me, that he must return to the cell and adopt an attitude which will reflect God's wrath. Would any advise that I should have done so?

Yet, there will be some people who will say by press or radio (can we doubt it?) that however long Alan remains in prison they can never, never forgive him for what he has done to that child. This is understandable and may be preferable to indifference; even so, a deep-seated self-righteousness is revealed in such attitudes. And if they truly mean what they say, and mean it to the end, then it is they who must one day be rejected and not Alan. Heaven is for Alan – there will be a lot of suffering on the way, as for all of us in the way of deepening self-knowledge – if he accepts God's forgiveness and perseveres to the end. And since you cannot have unforgivingness in heaven (it would cease to be heaven if you could) then it is I who have to be cast out if I cannot forgive. People who may think they are taking a fine and noble stand when they say they can never forgive so-and-so, naming

perhaps some notorious murderer, forget that their very statement, if they truly mean it, and if they remain that way, consigns
them and not the criminal to eternal death. The one clause in the
Lord's Prayer with a condition attached is 'forgive us our sins';
and, as if to emphasize its importance, a warning is given at the
end: 'If you do not forgive men their sins neither will your
heavenly father forgive your sins.'[7] God will not, not because he
is wilful or stubborn, but because he cannot. Not even God can
have an unforgiving soul in heaven and keep it heaven. The
kingdom of unforgivingness is the kingdom of hell. If by some
miracle the souls in hell could forgive one another it would be
immediately transformed into heaven. It is interesting to note
that, at the end of the Lord's Prayer, Jesus did not say that God's
forgiveness would be given to those who repented but to those
who forgave others. Ultimately it must be that the two things are
one and the same.

But what a difference, too, it makes in my attitude towards
myself if I believe there can be no anger in God! Anger towards
myself is a destructive emotion (self-anger and depression are
often closely related), yet what right have I not to exercise it
unless I am convinced that there is no anger in God which can be
directed towards me? And if such anger can indeed exist, it surely
must be resting on me, for who can say that even in the last few
minutes, let alone the last day, there has not been some thought,
omission, idleness or deed displeasing to an all-holy God whose
wrath may be incurred?

But we can look at this at a deeper level too. Largely through
the writings of C. G. Jung, we have become aware of a shadow
side of ourselves standing for the darker element of our nature
which it is difficult for us to acknowledge even to ourselves. It is,
consequently, easy for us to reject or disown this part of us;
whereas we have to learn to accept it and allow it to offer up to
the whole person whatever is good within it that it may be inte-
grated with the conscious life, making for a fuller and more
complete man or woman in Christ. The Christian who believes in
a God capable of wrath will believe that here in this darker area
of his life God's wrath will find the material on which it may be
supremely exercised. Hence, in so far as he is a God-fearing and
conscientious person he will tend to shut down the lid tightly on
it. If, however, there be no wrath in God, but only a loving
compassion, he will not be fearful to face this area in the power

of the Holy Spirit and allow it to be exposed. The way is thus opened for integration and healing to take place. I believe it to be true that if ever we are to grow into full maturity in Christ, it is essential that we eventually come to believe that there is no wrath in God. I would add that we are to let the Holy Spirit take us to that point in his own time. To believe the right thing at the wrong time is (for the person concerned) to believe the wrong thing.

What are we to say of anger as we meet it at the human level? Anger is a basic human emotion and to repress it or refuse to recognize it, perhaps because we fear it, will result in our driving it inward on ourselves, there to work out all sorts of havoc in our lives. 'Always be angry with God and not yourself,' someone once told me. 'He can take it and you can't.' It was shrewd advice and a strategy the psalm writers discovered nearly three thousand years ago. I suspect that much neurosis was saved thereby. But there are circumstances in life in which controlled anger may be at least a relative good in that it marks an advance on the alternative which may be indifference or cowardice. Controlled anger may be likened to a fire burning in the grate, uncontrolled anger to a forest fire. The one plays a useful part; the other destroys everything in its way. The one is our servant; the other our master. The one fulfils the Pauline injunction, 'Be angry but do not sin';[8] the other illustrates the meaning of James, 'The wrath of man worketh not the righteousness of God.'[9]

But what of Jesus? In the Authorised Version of the Bible (AV) he is made to say: 'Whosoever is angry with his brother without a cause shall be in danger . . .'[10] It is freely acknowledged that the words 'without a cause' are a later gloss, for the earlier extant manuscripts do not contain them. We shall therefore exclude them.

Let us note that Jesus did not say 'Don't be angry,' but 'If you are angry, this will follow . . .' There is an important difference between a notice which says 'No bathing' and one which reads 'The currents are dangerous'. It is with the latter that we are concerned. Bathing is at our own risk.

Alone among the translations which I am able to consult, the New English Bible (NEB) has: 'Anyone who *nurses* [my italics] his anger against his brother must be brought to judgement.' While we shall not doubt the truth of this, we may question

whether it was what Jesus was saying. It is somewhat obvious –
as, too, the earlier-mentioned glossed passage – and Jesus was
not given to uttering platitudes. It seems to me that the other
versions are to be preferred. In terms of our coastguard illustration
I think Jesus was saying: 'Bathe here if you have to, but look
out!'

However, we must go deeper than this. What we have said
applies simply at the level of conduct. What we are is of more
importance than what we do. As we grow in Christ the emotion
of anger undergoes transformation into righteousness. 'Blessed
are those who hunger and thirst after righteousness.' The passion
for righteousness may be illustrated in a man or woman who
embraces a cause such as prison reform or sheltering the homeless.
Yet only the few can work in such ways and we are all called to
the task which this saying of Jesus sets before us. When our life
is so motivated that it is lived for God's sake and not our own,
the hungering and thirsting after righteousness is contained within
every activity in the way of vocation, whether it be the housewife
faithful in cooking the children's meals or the monk or nun faithful
in the divine Office. Prayer is in fact the most powerful means
through which the passion of anger may be transformed. As coal
gives up its substance to become fire, so, in the power of the
Holy Spirit, anger surrenders its life to burn as the flame of
righteousness. If we do not like the word righteousness we could,
if we prefer, substitute holy or righteous love.

Symeon, the New Theologian, speaks of this transformation in
the following words:

> To be in control of one's temper and anger belongs to a wond-
> rous struggle and extreme effort, but to obtain to their complete
> quiescence and obtain serenity of heart and perfect gentleness
> is an act of God alone and a transformation at his hand.[11]

This transformation will not come through repression in its
psychological sense; the controlled expression of an instinct is the
forerunner to its sublimation. The important point to grasp, as I
see it, is that whereas in man the transformation of anger is a
continual process as he grows in the stature of Christ, in God (if
we may speak foolishly) it has never needed to take place for it
was there from the beginning. We in our varying states of wrath
are in the process of becoming what God has always been. When
we 'arrive' there will be no wrath in us as now there is no wrath

in God. In the stage of the young child it is all temper and tantrums; in the mature Christian it is holy love or that temper of life which Symeon describes. Meanwhile we are somewhere in between and rather than cowardly avoiding what in certain circumstances may be a Christian duty, we have to get along as well as we can in our intermediate and imperfect state with Paul's sane and practical advice to be angry but not to sin. A guideline for such anger will be that it is controlled and not 'nursed'. 'Let not the sun go down upon your wrath.'[12] It will also be as free from bitterness and hostility as our spiritual development allows. It would be unrealistic to pretend that these elements are not there in some degree, for righteousness as it exists in God can only fully 'take over' when we are well grown into the stature of Christ.

Righteousness is an aspect of love. Love may be likened to 'white' light which can be split into the various colours of the spectrum. Joy, peace, goodness, patience, righteousness and more are all 'colours' of the spectrum of love and are contained in harmony within the totality of love. Righteousness, needless to say, is not to be confused with self-righteousness which is a cancer of the soul. The righteous man is compassionate; the self-righteous is harshly judgemental. Perhaps it was in fear of that confusion that Paul did not include it in his famous list of the fruits of the Spirit.[13] That he considered it to be so is abundantly clear from his other writings. 'The kingdom of God', he writes, to take but one example, 'is not meat and drink; but righteousness, and peace, and joy in the Holy Ghost.'[14]

Notes

1 The page numbers refer to *William Law*, published by SPCK in 'The Western Classics of Spirituality' series 1980. The book contains *A Serious Call to a Devout and Holy Life* and *The Spirit of Love*.

2 *Julian of Norwich. Showings*, ch. 61.

3 Ibid., ch. 71.

4 A certain kind of Marian piety sees God or Christ as angry at the sins of man, ready indeed to destroy the world, yet restrained by the prayers of Mary, the compassionate mother. Sometimes theologians bring their heavy artillery to bear on this kind of pious fancy, yet it is surely worthy of sympathetic consideration against the background of the God of wrath and reprobation. That there should be somewhere

within the portals of judgment and vengeance a bearer of uncondi-
tional compassion is no small consolation to saint and sinner alike.
Anyhow, Julian places the all-compassionate figure within the
godhead, identifies it indeed with God's own countenance.' (From
Heaven in Ordinarie by Noel Dermot O'Donoghue. Edinburgh T. &
T. Clark 1979.)

5 I have deliberately chosen a fictitious name. It was delightfully
supplied to me by a printer in India who rendered a part of a service
sheet as: 'Our help is in the name of the Lord: Oho hath made heaven
and earth.'

6 I am reminded of an elderly Hindu who, after hearing Dr Stanley
Jones proclaim Christ to a mixed audience, thanked him with the
words: 'Sir, I have known him all my life; and now you have told me
his name.'

7 Matthew 6:15.

8 Ephesians 4:26 (RSV).

9 James 1:20 (AV).

10 Matthew 5:22 (AV).

11 *Symeon, The New Theologian: The Discourses*, trans. C. J. de Catan-
zaro. SPCK, 'The Western Classics of Spirituality' series.

12 Ephesians 4:26 (AV).

13 Galatians 5:22–3.

14 Romans 14:17 (AV).

Note on the anger of Jesus Anger in its unredeemed human state contains
within it elements such as bitterness, resentment, scorn, vindictiveness,
intemperance, malice, impatience, unforgivingness, and the like. As a
person grows under the sanctifying action of the Holy Spirit anger is
purged of these lower elements. It may be held that in ourselves this
process is never completed in this life. Only in the life of Jesus, it may
be said, has anger been completely purged of the elements which debase
it.

Since the anger of Jesus is so unlike anger as ordinarily encountered
it may be thought better to give it, and all anger purged or nearly purged
of its dross, a new name such as 'righteousness' as used in the text. If
we regard anger as being necessarily associated with its debasing elements
that might indeed be best. On the other hand by retaining the word
'anger' (as in 'righteous anger') we are recognizing the continuity of what
we find in Jesus with the unpurged activity belonging to our fallen state.

Whether we retain the word anger or opt for something else – the
energy of holy love or the flame of righteousness, or soul-force (to borrow
an Indian term) – the form used is less important than our understanding
of the meaning conveyed.

3

How about the Bible?

We must now apply ourselves to the second question. How about the Bible? Do we not read there again and again of the anger of God? We certainly do, and especially in the Old Testament. What may we say about that?

To begin with, we must note that in the Old Testament God's anger is linked with ethical concern. There is, supposedly, good objective reason for it such as man's rebellion, disobedience, flagrant injustice, exploitation of the weak, and so on. It is, however, well to add that in many cases where God's anger is said to be active, the mention of his mercy is not far away.

We may, I think, say this. From anger attributed to God, whether rightly or wrongly, there flow several good effects. To say that God is capable of anger keeps prominent the idea that he is a living God and one who is personally interested in our welfare. It also helps to keep alive the awareness of God's holiness and his abhorrence of evil, and it helps to preserve the truth that the wilful and persistent rejection of God must lead in the end to our own destruction. These are important truths and the Old Testament has preserved them by positing a God capable of wrath.

If we lose the concept of anger, must we lose too the concept of a living God who passionately desires that men and women shall be rescued from the spiritual darkness into which their evil inclinations are leading them? Would, perhaps, a concept other than anger – grief, for example – do instead? Certainly that may be so at the human level. It was his mother's tears and not her anger which brought St Augustine to repentance and life.

I think, myself, that we are to see anger in God, as portrayed in the Old Testament, as a relative truth, valuable – perhaps one should say vital – for a period in preserving the concepts of God to which we have referred, and acting as a preparation for a later revelation when Israel had been prepared to receive it. We are familiar both in history and in our everyday affairs with the distinction between what we may call relative and absolute truth. The sacrificial system of the Old Testament, for example, declared a relative truth which had to be surrendered in the light of the fuller revelation of the New. In the same way, in the Christian era, theories of the atonement have offered a relative truth preserving important values such as the holiness of God, the seriousness of sin, and the 'costingness' of forgiveness. Even though they may be at one point or another theologically defective – presenting, to take one example, Christ's suffering as being necessary to placate the displeasure of an angry God – they are not to be lightly dismissed, having served a purpose for a while, and perhaps for some serving a purpose still. At a more everyday level, the doctor explaining his diagnosis to a patient speaks in relative terms, reserving 'absolute' truth for his medical colleague who can understand the complexities involved. The father giving sex instruction to his ten-year-old boy knows that what can be said must be relative to the child's partial understanding at the time. So, to return to the Old Testament, we find repeatedly that God's revelation of himself, and a God who is angry on occasions is a part of that revelation, while authentic in the setting in which it was given, and serving a temporary purpose suited to the circumstances and understanding of the time, is none the less true only in a relative sense and needs to be corrected by the fuller insights of the Christian faith. This principle of progressive revelation according to our capacity to understand is for ever set before us in the words of Jesus to his disciples: 'I have many things to say to you but you cannot bear them now.' Not only does the Holy Spirit speak these words continually to his Church, but we apply them repeatedly in our converse with one another, as the above examples, which might be indefinitely multiplied, will suggest.

I think, however, that the question might be approached more profitably from a psychological angle. For this I shall need an analogy. Yesterday I was shown three portraits of a friend painted by three artists. They were all made at the same sitting by artists whose technical skill I shall assume to be equal. Here, then, we have a subject S painted by A1, A2, A3. On each canvas you never have plain S. On the first you have S as mixed up in the mind and personality of A1; we call it SA1. So, too we have SA2 and SA3. The image of S formed on the retinas of all three artists was (for our purpose) the same, but what was 'seen' was not the

image but its interpretation by one or other of them. Hence the marked differences which the canvases revealed.

Translating the analogy, a man of wrath, M, will tend to 'see' God, G, in some degree after M's likeness. Thus we never have G but always GM and we are all somewhere in the series GM1, GM2, and so on. If I, as one in the series, say that I feel it in my bones that God is angry I have to reflect that that need not be because of anything in God, but of something in 'my bones' and the only way forward is to make the leap of faith that God is not in fact what 'my bones' interpret him to be. This I can do because of the revelation of Calvary. As a man of wrath myself I shall always see God as angry (or capable of anger) unless I exercise this faith, or until my own wrath is quenched. Hence, those in Old Testament times were bound to regard God as wrathful since they were without any revelation of the nature open to later generations. As the artists could never see plain S but only SA, so they could never see plain G but only GM. Move into human relationships and you may say that a man, (M) never sees his neighbour, (N). He sees only NM and so our same neighbour becomes to us NM1, NM2, and so on, according to whom we are.[1]

When we come to the Epistles of the New Testament we must note some development and modification of the position of the Old. St Paul, for example, does indeed speak of 'the wrath of God' descending upon the children of disobedience, and yet that phrase occurs only three times in his Epistles. Many more times another phrase occurs, simply 'the wrath', standing as some would say for something impersonal. It is, in their view, as though one might say of a gambler or a swindler: 'Well, the day of reckoning had to come'; or, as someone in St Paul's day might have said, 'He couldn't in the long run escape the wrath.' In neither case would it necessarily be implied that God was angry. Professor C. H. Dodd in his commentary on the Letter to the Romans interprets Paul as understanding 'the wrath' entirely in this impersonal sense. He writes: '[Paul] retains the concept of "The Wrath of God" not to describe the attitude of God to man, but to describe the inevitable process of cause and effect in a moral universe.' In support of his view Dodd observes that Paul never uses the verb 'to be angry' with God as subject. He points out that Paul speaks of the love of God and that he says that God loves us; that he

speaks of the graciousness of God and that he says God is gracious; that he speaks of the faithfulness of God and that he says God is faithful; but that although he speaks of the wrath of God he never says that God is angry. Dodd continues: 'We cannot attribute to God the irrational passion of anger.'[2]

How are we to regard Dodd's view? For myself I welcome his observation that Paul never says in so many words that God is angry (and perhaps, if pressed, Paul would have refused to commit himself in this way), and I welcome further his assertion that the irrational passion of anger cannot be attributed to God. The first – that Paul is never on record as saying that God is angry – is a statement beyond dispute and the second is an expression of Dodd's personal belief. For the rest it must be left to New Testament scholars to decide whether Paul would have shared Dodd's views. I think myself that while Paul would not have disagreed with Dodd's statement that the wrath of God may be understood as 'the inevitable process of cause and effect in a moral universe', he would also not have been content with it. He would have been discontented not because he regarded it as false but because he regarded it as expressing a secondary rather than a primary truth. The Jew in Paul must always have taken him back and back to God who was behind all. Paul would have rejoined, 'But who made this universe? And who made it moral? Who made it to operate in accordance with certain physical and spiritual laws?' And the answer, of course, is God. Hence the wrath which overtakes 'the children of disobedience', while in a secondary sense it is the working out of the inbuilt laws of the universe, would have been seen by Paul (it seems possible to me) also in its primary sense, that is to say in the area of the personal. And, *perhaps*, this would have made it possible for Paul to say plainly on occasions that 'God is angry', even though he is not recorded as having done so.

This is speculation only. One welcomes Dodd's personal beliefs and one hopes that he is right in his belief that Paul shared them. Otherwise we would be faced between Dodd (and Julian) on the one hand and Paul on the other. Dodd does not believe that that choice has to be made. He believes that we can be with him and Paul at the same time. But critics are not wanting in thinking that that is not so.

There is no reference to God's anger in the teaching of Jesus

unless (in the words of Professor Dodd) 'we press certain features of the parables in an illegitimate manner'.[3] There is, however, in the Gospels, one reference to 'the wrath of God' (John 3:36), though whether these words belong to John the Baptist, or are to be seen as a commentary by the Gospel writer on the earlier words of the Baptist, is not clear. Certainly it would not seem inappropriate to attribute the phrase to the Baptist, who is earlier reported by Matthew and Luke to have spoken of 'the wrath' (though in an impersonal sense, as we saw of Paul on a number of occasions): 'Who hath warned you to flee from the wrath to come?' Commentators, however, incline to the view that the phrase belongs to the Gospel writer whom many believe to have been John the beloved disciple. If that be so, it will be interesting to reflect that John himself was reputedly of a fiery nature. Together with his brother James he had been nicknamed Boanerges – sons of thunder – and again, with James, he had wanted to call down fire from heaven to burn up some Samaritan villagers who had refused to offer hospitality to Jesus and his disciples.[4] The rebuke which he received showed how little he then understood of the mind of Jesus, and would appear to offer evidence of how Jesus dissociated himself from what is likely to have been the popular conception of the wrath of God in action. It is true that John was writing his Gospel more than half a century later. Even so, the dispositions of youth die hard and it may be that much of his old fiery temperament remained. Professor Barclay relates a story from Eusebius telling how John, on learning that the heretic Cerinthus was sharing a bath house with him, fled from the building, calling to his companions: 'Let us flee, lest the bath fall, for Cerinthus the enemy of truth is within.' It would not, it seems, have been thought unfitting if God had dealt thus with his enemies.[5]

Turning to the Gospel text, the words to which we have referred are: 'He who puts his faith in the Son has hold of eternal life, but he who disobeys the Son shall not see that life: God's wrath rests upon him.' William Temple, in his *Readings in St John's Gospel*,[6] comments especially on the last five words. He writes:

Terrible words. A sentimental and hedonist generation tries to eliminate 'wrath' from its conception of God. Of course if 'anger' and 'wrath' are taken to mean the emotional reaction of an irritated self-concern, there is no such thing in God. But

if God is holy love, and I am in any degree given to uncleanness
or selfishness, then there is, in that degree, stark antagonism in
God against me.

It will be seen that Temple, while upholding the conception of
wrath in God, warns us that it is to be understood differently from
anger or wrath as we commonly meet it in ourselves. At the
human level there is liable to be an outburst of irritation or
annoyance, of fury or rage, which has little or even nothing to do
with the ethical demands of the situation which confronts us, but
a great deal to do with a corruption within ourselves. It may be
that our pride has been wounded or our vanity pricked, our
convenience threatened or our selfish concerns frustrated, and we
break out in angry protest. Thus, we are much more liable to
show annoyance or rage when someone provokes ourselves or our
family than when a similar provocation is offered to a household
in the next street. All such thinking is to be eliminated when we
come to consider wrath in God. The annoyance or 'anger' side
will still be there – it seems that Temple is saying this (controlled,
we naturally assume) – but there will be a purity of motive and
an absence of selfish concern such as we seldom, if ever, find at
the human level.

We have here in Temple's comment the two elements of God's
wrath which the Book of Common Prayer sets before us.
Following this rite we are bidden at every Eucharist to acknowledge that we have provoked God's 'wrath and indignation against
us'. The first three words of the quotation present us with what
we have called the annoyance side of God's wrath, and the last
two of the antagonistic or opposition side of which Temple chiefly
speaks. I suppose it is true that most Anglican church people have
gone along with that conception, often unquestioningly, for most
of their lives. For myself, it never occurred to me in earlier years
to question Temple's comment. I can, however, no longer believe
that in so far as I am given to uncleanness or selfishness there is,
in that degree, stark antagonism in God towards me. Even if the
annoyance side of the conception of God's wrath were to be
eliminated as being too anthropomorphic to fasten on to God,
this, the antagonistic side, would remain. And that – I have to own
through Julian – I am not able to accept.[7] The gospel according to
Julian as she writes for her 'even-Christians' is not simply that
God is that goodness which cannot be angry (in the sense of

annoyance, rage, etc.) but that he is on our side even when we are sinning. God is never to be seen as being antagonistic or opposed to us but always as one who would draw us to himself by the goodness of mercy and grace. 'The wrath of God', if I may quote the best definition which I know, 'is his relentless compassion pursuing us when we are at our worst'.[8]

I have to confess – I hope with every reader – that there is within me a degree of uncleanness or selfishness, and that that will remain so until the end. Even if we were writing of the saints it seems to me that that would be true. Are we then, as Christians, whoever we may be, to live throughout our lives with a God who in some degree is antagonistic towards us? If, as Jesus says, we are not to resist the one who wrongs us (an ideal, no doubt, which we seldom reach) why should we expect God to have a lesser standard than man?

Wrath opposes; it is, as Temple indicates, of the nature of wrath to oppose. Sometimes it is argued that God in his wrath is to be seen as opposing the sin but not the sinner. But sin is an abstraction; it cannot exist on its own. There is no such thing as sin; there is only a person sinning. Murder and (unintentional) homicide can be made to look identical as far as the outward act is concerned; it is the presence or absence of evil intent which distinguishes one from the other. The sin is strictly to be found not in the deed but in the evil will which lies behind the deed. Could it then be my evil will which God opposes? No, because once again 'will' – though I have just found it convenient to use the word – is an abstraction. There is no such thing as 'will' (though the concept is useful) but only a person 'willing'. So it is me whom a God capable of wrath must oppose. If you believe in a God who can be angry you must believe that there will be occasions when he opposes you: you yourself, not your sin nor your sinful will (both of which are abstractions) but simply you. On the other hand, if you believe with Julian that God is incapable of anger, then you may believe with her that God is on your side even when you are sinning. The first image will satisfy only in what we have earlier regarded as a limited and relative sense; in an absolute sense it will not do.

But, it may be said, Julian stands alone, or almost so. She did so once, but today the theological climate has changed which is partly why she can speak so clearly across the centuries. Let me give one example, which cannot be without great significance. In

the Alternative Service Book (ASB) of 1980 there is a service of
Holy Communion (pp. 146ff.) entitled 'The Order following the
pattern of the Book of Common Prayer'. In this service the
congregation is offered four possible general confessions, of which
not one offers the 'wrath and indignation' clause of the pattern
which the service professes to follow. I see this as evidence of a
right development and not of a 'hedonist and sentimental'
theology which we would be right to fear.

The word 'antagonism' provokes in me the wrong image by
which I may understand God's dealing with us. If a room is in
darkness you do not meet the situation by opposing the darkness;
rather do you draw back the curtains and let in the light. So, in
our state of darkness or semi-darkness, God is not to be seen in
opposition but rather, as it were, at the curtains, though drawing
them back slowly, slowly so as not to give our eyes more pain
than they can be expected to bear. The picture is not original; it
is in fact taken from John himself. In the first chapter of his
Gospel he speaks of the light of Christ shining in the darkness, a
light which the darkness is unable to quench. William Law
expresses this thought magnificently in these words:

> The spirit of love does not want to be rewarded, honored or
> esteemed. Its only desire is to propagate itself and become the
> blessing and happiness of everything that wants it. And there-
> fore it meets wrath and evil and hatred and opposition with the
> same one will as the light meets the darkness, only to overcome
> it with all its blessings. Did you want to avoid the wrath and ill
> will or to gain the favor of any persons, you might easily miss
> of your ends; but if you have no will but to all goodness,
> everything you meet, be it what it will, must be forced to be
> assistant to you. For the wrath of an enemy, the treachery of a
> friend and every other evil only helps the spirit of love to be
> more triumphant, to live its own life and find its own blessings
> in a higher degree.[9]

God himself is the Spirit of love and here we have portrayed the
action of God in relation to man. He meets us as light meets
darkness, not in the way of antagonism but in the desire to overcome the darkness with all the blessings which light may bring.
The picture is not one of antagonism whereby God opposes us
until we are purged of uncleanness or selfishness but one which
portrays God as being on our side even when we are but partially

cleansed – as must always be the case – of our sins. If we may return to a Julian quotation we have already used: 'In the time of our sinning he shows to us the demeanour of ruth and pity, mightily protecting and defending us against all our enemies.' As a priest I am assured of how many of Julian's 'even-Christians' need with me this message of comfort and hope. 'Our courteous Lord does not want his servants to despair because they fall often and grievously; for our falling does not hinder him in loving us.'[10] Such a quotation by no means takes the truth out of such texts as 'whom the Lord loveth he chasteneth'. Julian's writing is rich in allusions to the chastening love of God, but God's chastening is never the wrath by which he would oppose us but the love through which he would draw us. And this, of course, is faithful to the insight of the New Testament.

It may be that we can be helped in our understanding if we consider an example in human relationships. I think of the attempt on the life of Pope John Paul. On the one hand we have the man who attacked him, defiantly unrepentant and proclaiming bitterly as he is led from one prison to another that his one regret is that his assassination attempt has failed. On the other, we hear the Pope saying from his hospital bed that he has already forgiven his assailant, that he bears no ill will or bitterness towards him, and that he holds him in his prayers. Can one not say without straining of language that the Pope is on the side of his assailant even while this man remains hostile and impenitent; on his side, drawing him in love towards penitence and reconciliation? And then when, some months later, the two meet in a prison cell and (there is reason to conjecture) the man expresses sorrow and asks for forgiveness, the Pope does not even have to forgive but merely has to assure the man of the forgiveness which has been present all the time, but which may now become fully operative because the other's heart is open to receive it. Raise that example to the level of God and man and we have Calvary's picture of God's dealing with us. The forgiveness of Jesus from the cross preceded the movement towards sorrow and penitence which would enable it to be fully operative.

The word opposition is generally used in the sense of antagonism and carries with it overtones of wrath. Yet it can be used in quite a different sense, as when a man who turns the other cheek can be said to oppose evil with good. As God cannot do less than he asks of a good man, it is in this sense that he may rightly be said to oppose evil. Julian herself uses the word of God in this manner, writing that 'the property of God which opposes good to evil' is the 'goodness of mercy and grace'.[11] This is the overcoming of evil with good of which Paul speaks and is not opposition in the sense in which that word is generally understood. Julian, I suspect, is wanting to bring out a contrast, saying in effect: 'God doesn't oppose evil with wrath, but I will tell you how he does oppose it – with "the goodness of mercy and grace".' In this way, the Pope, in the example just given, may be said to have opposed evil, drawing its sting with mercy and grace.

In the garden of Gethsemane the disciples had two swords and Peter used one of them to attack the group which came to arrest Jesus. It was a noble outburst of rage and it stood higher in the scale of moral values than indifference or cowardice. But there was a third sword at the Passion and, as Simeon had prophesied, it pierced the Virgin Mother's heart. She suffered as none other at the treatment accorded her son. It is not in the anger of Peter, noble as that in its setting may have been, but in the patience and longsuffering of Mary that we are brought to the very heart of God. And in the outstretched arms upon the cross, reaching out in compassion to those who laid him bare, we come to the central revelation of God's love. There is no element of wrath, whether in the Father or the Son, which troubles the hilltop of Calvary. Rather do we see here, following the thought of Julian, that, as we contemplate the compassionate figure on the cross, we come to know that the wrath which is 'within us' is being 'abated and dispelled' by the mercy and forgiveness of God.[12]

Notes

1 The argument has been delightfully illustrated by our (then) eight-year-old server whose mother tells me that when a tremendous thunderstorm burst just before a friend's wedding, he commented: 'God is angry because she is using his church for the wedding and she doesn't go at other times.' One's first reaction may be 'Out of the mouths of babes . . .'! But more seriously, his observation well supports the argument in the text. This is what he would have done!
2 See *The Epistle of Paul to the Romans*, in the Moffatt New Testament Commentary series. See the commentary on Romans 1:18;
3 See again the commentary on Romans 1:18 in the book cited above.

4 Luke 9:52–6.

5 The story is taken from William Barclay, *The Gospel of St John,* vol. 1. Edinburgh, The Saint Andrew Press 1955. See page xxiv. (Barclay's reference to Eusebius is 3:28.)

6 *Readings in St John's Gospel* by William Temple. Macmillan 1939.

7 This is not to deny that the deliberate and persistent rejection of love must always lead to a deepening of corruption within. If we choose to describe this working out of a spiritual law ('a man reaps what he sows') as 'the wrath' (or 'the wrath of God' if we want to make the point dramatically by personalizing what is really impersonal) in action within, there is nothing to prevent us from doing so. The point the text is concerned to make is that the waters from the fountain always pour forth fresh and clear and that there is nothing within man which can corrupt them ('turn them into wrath') at their source.

8 *The Fire of Your Life* by Maggie Ross. Paulist Press.

9 *William Law. A Serious Call to a Devout and Holy Life – The Spirit of Love.* SPCK, 'The Western Classics of Spirituality' series, p. 359.

10 *Julian of Norwich. Showings*, ch. 39.

11 Ibid., ch. 59.

12 Ibid., ch. 48. 'I was forced to agree that the mercy of God and his forgiveness abate and dispel our wrath'.

General chapter note. To allay possible misunderstanding it needs, perhaps, to be affirmed that in the traditional view of the Church (encapsulated by Temple, to whom I owe so much) God's anger in no way contradicts his love; in the final analysis God is always acting for us. To say this does not, of course, affect the basic distinction between tradition and Julian for whom the wrath is seen to be in us and not in God. Whilst the relative truth (of tradition), which sees the wrath to be in God, may serve for a while, only the 'absolute' truth (of Julian) can ultimately satisfy.

Part Two

Man's Response

4

Laying the Foundations

We have considered the compassionate nature of God's love following us into every situation and never deserting us however grievously we may fall away from him. In this we have drawn extensively on the insights of Julian who would have us know that even in the time of our sinning God's compassion and pity are present to strengthen and encourage us. 'For love never allows him to be without pity; and when we fall into sin, and neglect recollection of him and the protection of our own soul, then Christ bears all alone the burden of us.'[1] This insight of Julian's, rooted in the gospel, though not always discovered there, that 'during the time that we are in sin . . . he waits for us and does not change his demeanour . . .'[2] is one we need to have before us as we come to consider our response to God in the way of prayer. Our waywardness and our frailty are not to discourage us, since our hope is not in ourselves but in the constancy of God's love. Our greatest enemy is likely to be neither our temperament nor our environment nor our sins – none of these *in themselves*, but the discouragement to which they may give rise. If we hold fast at that point, there is nothing God cannot do for us.

Our prayer life, then, is to be seen at every point as a response to the beckoning, calling, yearning love of God. It is good to remember as we go to prayer that God is always on the scene first; in every situation he is there waiting for us, his arms are outstretched to us before we ever turn to him. Prayer is the movement of myself, the whole of me, the body–soul–spirit structure which identifies me as me, towards the welcoming arms of God. In this movement freely made my heart is opened towards God, as any man or woman's heart is opened to their lover, and in the healing power of love to which the prayer life lays me open, resistances are broken down, prejudices are overcome, passions are subdued, fears are dissolved, memories are healed, relationships are enlarged, and a new spirit comes to irradiate my life which becomes increasingly marked with the note of trustfulness and thanksgiving, and that independently – we are speaking of the perfect work which we see realized in the lives of the saints – of whether the outward circumstances of life are favourable or not. This is not just rhetoric, it is the plain truth of what the Holy Spirit works in us as day by day our offering is renewed in the work of prayer. It is true that as we look at ourselves we seem to have come a very little way. We are not, however, speaking of the work of a moment nor of five years nor even of ten. It is the work of a lifetime – and more – and basically it is what life is all about. It may not be a bad thing from time to time to take a look at the mountain peak even though it seems to us we are no further than the foothills, and that what we most need is practical help on how to make the journey.

We shall come to this in some detail later on. But first we may note a number of points which are to be borne in mind as we seek the deepening of our prayer life. If it seems at times in the succeeding chapters that any of these are overlooked, that must be reckoned as an appearance only. We can give our attention only to one thing at a time; yet we must remember that the considerations which follow are to govern everything we shall say of the life of prayer.

Our first consideration is this. Life must be taken and accepted as a whole, and prayer can never be separated from daily living. Such a statement, while not in dispute, may provoke the challenge that we should define our terms, making it clear in what sense we are to understand prayer. A great Christian thinker in the early days of the Church has a famous phrase which speaks of life as 'one great unbroken prayer',[3] and that is to be seen as the ideal, however far it may now be from being a reality. Prayer would then include cooking meals, visiting the sick, mending the garden fence, answering the telephone, eating and drinking and sleeping and all. There can be no theoretical objection to extending the meaning of prayer in this way. To make prayer coextensive with life itself is how it should be and how it has been in the lives of some. Brother Lawrence was wont to say that all perfection was contained in such a simple act as picking up a straw from the ground if only it could be done solely for the love of God.

If, however, for our present purpose I were thus to regard prayer, the book would have to be extended to take account of the whole range of Christian living rather than of some specific activity within it. I shall, therefore, for our present need, define prayer as that activity in which we are engaged, when alone or in the company of others, our hearts and minds and wills are occupied with God and him alone. And I shall regard Christian activity whether religious, so-called, or secular, so-called, as the overspill of prayer into daily life. God is indeed to be glorified in the whole of our lives but the only way in which there is the remotest chance that that may one day be so, is through our taking regular times in which he alone is sought and in which every motive other than the glory of God is, as far as possible, put away. It will be good to reflect in passing that God does not value our prayer time because it is in itself more valuable than any other time, but because all time is meant to become charged with the meaning of this particular time. But how shall this be? The answer is simple, at least in theory, and has been neatly summarized in these words by John Dalrymple: 'You will never be able to pray everywhere all the time until you have first learnt to pray somewhere some of the time.'[4]

But in so limiting prayer we are to stress, as we have seen, that it is never to be disengaged from the total offering of life. It is the possibility that this may happen and sometimes has happened that has often brought the subject of prayer into disrepute. Prayer and living will be continually acting and reacting on one another. Ultimately each side of life will move towards completion supported and supplemented by the other.

The second consideration – perhaps I should have put it first, there is no significance in the order – is this. We go to prayer, so far as it may be given us to do so, for God's sake and not our own.

Let us face it that in the beginning it is true of us all that we go to God largely for what we may hope to get out of him. It may be that we are worried about our sins and go to God for assurance and peace; or that we are anxious and depressed and turn to him for consolation and strength; or that a beloved friend is ill and we plead with God that his or her life may be spared to us for a while longer. The list could go on and on. We are not to despise such lowly movements towards God even though they are governed by a large measure of self-interest. God, like any good father, always takes us on from where we are, accepts our lower

motives and works through them to something better. But if,
having achieved our desire – the depression has lifted or the sick
friend has recovered – we then forget all about God as we had
done before, it is obvious that little or nothing of any religious
significance has taken place, and that the whole thing has been
little more than an exercise in manipulating God to achieve our
own ends.

The foregoing may well serve to illustrate what many are experi-
encing at a deeper level of the spiritual life. It commonly happens,
as every priest will know, that people who come to talk about their
prayer life will bring with them a problem which they describe
something like this: 'My prayer time has become very difficult.
My feelings and emotions seem to have gone dead on me. I find
in the silence little joy and refreshment and it is often nothing but
a grind. It wasn't always like that; in fact there was a time when
I looked forward to it. Nowadays I often make excuses to avoid
it.'

When people speak in that way it must be fairly clear that we
have here, repeated at a later stage in the spiritual life, the same
problem which we met before. Although we may have thought of
ourselves as going to God for his sake and not our own it is
evident that we have in some measure got it wrong. But this
should not discourage us. Instead of deploring our situation we
should welcome it, for not only does it mark a growth in self-
knowledge but it provides an opportunity for bringing to our
prayer a deeper purity of motive than was open to us before. It
is only when the consolations and conscious rewards are removed
and we are thrown back on to the nakedness of faith that the
quite basic question presents itself: what is my prayer life really
about? Is it about serving God and surrendering all to him? Is it
about submitting to God's will and abandoning my own will to
the work of the Holy Spirit? Is my prayer life about these things
or has it to do with some rather subtle form of self-seeking,
more respectable, no doubt, than the pursuit of wealth or the
entertaining of worldly ambitions but very likely more dangerous
as being more liable to self-deception? A crisis of the sort of which
we are speaking reveals the worth or otherwise of what has gone
before. An important lesson in the spiritual life is that we are not
to rest in its pleasant experiences as though in some sense they
belonged to us as of right, nor equally are we to seek them as if
they were of value simply for their own sake. We have to learn

to offer them or to hand them over to God and they then become as stepping-stones leading to deeper knowledge and a fuller union with him. When things go well it is all too easy to fall into the trap of trying to hold on to what we have. We are rather like Peter on the mountain of transfiguration. The vision was breathtaking and wonderful, so (says Peter) why not build three comfortable little huts, one for each of us, and we can settle down here for ever? His reaction would doubtless have been different if, instead of glory, there had been fog or howling wind and storm. And our reaction in prayer is likewise apt to be different if, instead of finding the consolations which usually mark the early stages of prayer, we find dryness, or, perhaps, persistent distractions or hostile forces such as fears and disturbing memories arising from within. But really this is our opportunity, for not only do we have to pass through this sort of country for God's healing work to be done within us, but the very troublesomeness of this type of experience encourages us to hand it over to God which is just what we ought to do. Then when we have passed through the wind and the rain, or it may be, to change the picture, the heat and dryness of the desert stretches, and fair weather once more is our lot, we have learnt through the handling of adverse conditions how to handle the good conditions as well, not by clutching them but by offering them. Speaking quite generally (and outside the prayer life in the restricted use of the words), I believe God would give us more joys if we knew how to manage them properly. Pleasant experiences, instead of leading to thanksgiving, easily become (but not at all necessarily so) the occasion of our sinking down into lethargy and self-indulgence. At first our situation seems to have the promise of life and vigour, but in the end it turns out to be one of boredom and weariness. Schoolchildren usually start their holidays full of energy, high hopes and high spirits, but by the time a few weeks have passed, their parents are likely to be saying it will be good for them to get back to their lessons again. The discipline of the term is demanding and sometimes unpleasant by contrast with the easygoing freedom of the holidays, but if the children can accept it and respond to it, it takes them to horizons they would not otherwise have discovered.

Life and prayer (now strictly understood) run on parallel lines here. All God's gifts are good and to be accepted gratefully but at the same time we are to be always moving beyond them to God himself who is greater than all his gifts, and in whom all his gifts are included. Julian's prayer, 'God, of your goodness give me yourself, for you are enough for me',[5] presents the ideal on which our sights are to be set. When we reach the crisis point to which we have referred, we have before us a new opportunity. The props on which we have relied are being knocked down one by one and we are left only with faith as our support. We cannot see much, perhaps we cannot see anything at all, and if we could then we would not be depending on faith alone. Certainly we ought not to be feeling guilty about what is taking place; on the contrary it is a normal development and one to be embraced. Soon we may have no feelings to reassure us, nor even any sure knowledge whether what we are doing is pleasing to God or not. Pure faith has been described as that state in which we serve God without any pledge or assurance that what we are doing is pleasing to him.[6] That does not at all suit the unregenerate man in us who is always seeking after assurances of one sort or another, whether externally in the form of signs or internally in the realm of feeling. Yet it is, we are assured, an evil and adulterous generation which seeks after a sign. We are now, then, thrown back on faith alone and until God chooses that it shall be otherwise, this is the one way forward, and in it we shall find the gradual undermining of our self-love and in the end its destruction as far as is possible in this life.

We can be one of two people in relation to our prayer life, though more accurately we are always a mixture of both. We can belong to the type who 'come wind, come weather' settle down to our appointed prayer time (Office, Jesus Prayer, silence, whatever it may be) and see it through, regardless of our mood or of whether it may seem to us to be useful or strengthening or comforting or anything else. Or we can be of the type which says that we do not feel much in the mood for praying today and in that case it won't do us any good even if we make the attempt. That we find both elements within each of us need not be a cause for despondency; the important thing to discover is which side is gaining ground. If it is the second then it is to be feared that we are building our house upon sand. It may for a while seem to have something to offer but when the floods come and the winds blow its flimsy foundations will be revealed.

No, no, it will not do to make our prayer time depend on mood and inclination. G. K. Chesterton once said that if a thing was worth doing it was worth doing badly. The paradox holds our

attention and although it cannot be applied as a general rule –
driving cars or folding parachutes are obvious examples – it can
offer something of great value in the realm of prayer. On those
days when I know it must be that I shall say my Office (or
whatever it is) with my mind a good deal scattered, I can say to
myself, 'Say it badly, say it as badly as you must, but for God's
sake (yes, literally, for God's sake) say it.' The chances are that
before ten minutes have passed some degree of recollection will
be taking over, but even if it is not so, it does not matter, since
we are engaged in this business for God's sake and not our own.
This is to be our offering and it is helpful to see it in that light.
The great thing about an offering is that it does not have to
'succeed'. It simply has to be offered and with such love and
gratitude as may be given us. It is of no matter if we do not feel
this love or gratitude; the important thing is to express it. It is
what we would like to feel if it were given us to do so. The will
often marches ahead of the feelings even though in the long run
the feelings catch up. Hence a golden rule is never to judge prayer
by how it seems to be at the time but by its later fruits. Just
because what is happening is at the level of the unconscious we
cannot, by definition, be aware of it. If we can grasp that, we
shall not be tempted to interrupt our prayer time with foolish
questions as to whether it is doing us any good or helping anybody
else. That is God's business and he wants us to attend to ours.

It is obvious that if it is given us to respond in the way we have
described, there will be a gradual putting to death of self-will.
Jesus tells us that it is in the losing of our life that we find it and
that is as true in the area of prayer – and perhaps more so – as
in the 'active' engagements of life. It is, however, worth noting
that Jesus did not say that we are to lose our life *in order that* we
may find it, although he is commonly misquoted as having done
so. He made simply the plain statement that if you do lose your
life you will in fact find it, or that if a corn of wheat falls into the
ground and dies it will bear much fruit. The difference is
important. In neither case is there any appeal to my enlightened
self-interest but, rather, an invitation to death and abandonment
'for my sake and the gospels' without regard to what the future
may hold. It is the Pauline phrase from the Authorised Version
(AV), 'dying and behold we live' which admirably throws light
on the words of Jesus. If we cut out the word 'behold' and make
the phrase read 'dying in order that we may live' it is at once clear

that we have lost a world of meaning. This is no calculated venture embarked upon because it is going to bring in rich returns. It is death and it seems like real death this time: down we go and all the waterfloods go over us, nothing to be won here, and then 'behold', surprise of surprises, we break surface again. It is that picture we have to take into our life generally and into our prayer life in particular. What is asked of us at some particular moment looks like loss, has every appearance of loss, and the plunge is taken. Jesus did not die on the cross in order that he might rise again. He died, was truly dead, and lo and behold (so it was to the disciples), 'God raised him'. In that thought there is a parable which has application to every aspect of the Christian life.

The third point to bear in mind as we approach the chapters on prayer is this: only the Holy Spirit can enable us to pray. I think it may be especially important to recall this point in the present climate of teaching in which we hear so much of the place of technique in prayer. Let me say at once that we are not to despise technique. We need it in everything we do, whether making a phone call or driving a car or simply walking down the street. The important thing to bear in mind about technique is that it must always occupy a subordinate place. The end of prayer is encounter or communion with God and the place of technique is to prepare the way for that encounter to take place. So long as we do not confuse the means with the end technique is to be welcomed and we may seek to profit by it. But let us remember how, in the words of St Augustine, we come to God by love and not by navigation and not even the best-drawn charts in the world can of themselves take us to the harbour where we would be.

So, then, however much help we may receive from books and people – and it would be foolish to neglect that help – it remains true that when we come to the making of prayer itself only the Holy Spirit can enable us. St Paul, it will be remembered, tells us that the Holy Spirit comes to our aid in our weakness, making intercession for us with groanings which cannot be uttered. My commentary paraphrases those words as 'inexpressible longings which God alone understands' and that seems to me to be a good description of contemplative prayer. Contemplation is indeed a gift, the gift of the Spirit, and only the Spirit can take us to it and lead us in it. It is probable that many readers have been called for some time to this way of prayer while others are on the threshold of it. It is a call to be awaited rather than sought, and if sought it should be gently sought in patience, abiding God's time rather than our own. The Spirit moves where he wills, and whether it be in vocal prayer, or in tongues (as it may be for some), or in the silence of contemplation, only he can enable us to pray.

Then, lastly, let me say a word about the nature of the silence we shall meet with in these pages. Broadly speaking, there is a silence of will-gathering and a silence of wool-gathering. In the former the faculties are gathered up in a generous and loving attention to God. There is an expectant waiting upon him whereby we may hear his voice in the depths of our being. By contrast the silence of wool-gathering is an absentminded daydreaming silence in which fancies may be indulged, resentments nursed, troubles bemoaned, vanities entertained and self-pityings cherished. To the outside observer the two silences may look alike. Yet the one perhaps is the most creative force in heaven and earth and it may be that the other is the most destructive. More destructive than the fouling of the material atmosphere by smells and fumes is the pollution of the psychic atmosphere by the poisonous stream of our negative and pernicious thoughts. True silence which is creative silence is the most demanding activity God asks of any of us. Here it is that heart and mind and will, memory and imagination are gathered up and collected in God. We ought to call that a state of collection. But strangely (at first sight) we call it a state of recollection, which strictly speaking should be pronounced *re*-collection. No doubt we use the word recollection because we are so often losing our collection, and so we are more conscious of becoming *re*-collected than of being collected.

In thinking of creative silence two images may be helpful. They should be taken together for neither is complete without the other. You could think of this silence, if you like, as the silence of a sentry on duty, seeing it in terms of alertness and awareness. These qualities are assisted in the sentry by the posture he adopts, and in the same way in prayer the posture we choose can be a help: it is in fact a part of the technique of which we have spoken earlier.

A further image is given by thinking of two people who deeply love one another, and describing silence in terms of understanding and perception and harmony. Here is the picture of a relaxed and loving silence, the sort of silence two friends might experience before the fire of a winter's evening, each being supported by the silent presence of the other, conversation being now superfluous, or at least being allowed to come and go quite freely as it will. Taken together, these images point us towards contemplative silence.

Notes

1 *Julian of Norwich. Showings*, ch. 80.
2 Ibid., ch. 78.
3 Origen (*c.* 185–254).
4 *The Christian Affirmation*. John Dalrymple. 1976.
5 *Julian of Norwich. Showings*, ch. 5.
6 The thought and that at the end of the paragraph belong to J. N. Grou. The full quotation may be found on page 67 of *The Dart of Longing Love*. Darton Longman and Todd 1983.

5

Psalming down the Devil[1]

I had considered starting this book with Baron von Hügel's parable of the wayside cow. On reflection, however, I have thought it belongs best at the head of this chapter, though I trust its message may be extended to all sections which demand the forbearance of its readers. The parable may be found as the closing section of one of von Hügel's letters to his niece.[2] He has been telling her not to force herself to see, nor yet to pretend to see, truths which are beyond her present grasp; but, equally, let her not decide that, because some principle or truth is now beyond her, it therefore does not exist, nor may not be one which she will come to hold later on. The parable runs:

I so love to watch cows as they browse at the borders, up against the hedges of fields. They move along, with their great tongues drawing in just only what they can assimilate; yes – but without stopping to snort defiantly against what does not thus suit them. It is as though these creatures had the good sense to realize that those plants which do not suit them – that these will be gladly used up by sheep, goats or horses; indeed that some of these plants may suit them – the cows themselves – later on. So ought we to do: not sniff and snort at what we do not understand here and now; not proclaim, as though it were a fact interesting to anyone but ourselves, that we do not, here and now, understand this or that thing; but we should just merely, quite quietly, let such things stand over, as possibly very true, though to us they look very foolish – as indeed possibly things that we ourselves will come to penetrate as true and right indeed. In a word, we can and should be sure of all that is positive and fruitful for us in our outlook; sure also that whatever really contradicts *that* is false. But as to further possible truths and facts, we will leave ourselves peacefully docile and open.

There it is, then. Cows won't eat buttercups but they thrive on swedes; thistles, I am told, they will eat only when cut. They are as choosy as the rest of us, but they know their needs and they nudge to one side, peacefully and gently, what is not suitable for present consumption. I ask the reader to do the same. No snorting defiantly, please!

I make these points because I want to devote this chapter to a form of prayer which is becoming of increasing importance to many people today, and yet is regarded by others with suspicion and sometimes with distaste. Even so, it has a very long history in the experience of the Church, both in the Orthodox Church and in the Roman Catholic Church, but, at least until recent years, a much lesser place in our Anglican tradition. I am speaking of repetitive prayer, usually in the form of a single short sentence said over and over again as a means of expressing and developing our aspirations towards God. The single sentence is not a necessary part of the pattern, and some prefer to use a psalm or part of a psalm, well tried and well loved, and (importantly) thoroughly committed to memory. Psalm 43 of the Book of Common Prayer ('Give sentence with me, O God . . .'), already known by heart to many older people, who at one time used it as the introit psalm at the Eucharist, makes an admirable recitation; as, too, do the first five verses of Psalm 103 ('Praise the Lord, O my soul . . .'). But, equally, the prayer or affirmation can be reduced all the way down to a single word such as Abba, Father, God, or Jesus. The Jesus Prayer, which we shall come to later, is often shortened to this one word, Jesus. It is likely to be that, as we become more accustomed to this way of prayer, the movement will be towards shortening rather than lengthening what we are to say. Yet, even then, I think that longer recitations may regularly meet our need best.

Whatever outward form we use, the practice begins largely at the level of the mind, but gradually the prayer descends to the heart and takes root there, and finally the words may die away as the heart remains at prayer. The words, pronounced aloud, also have the power of clearing the superficial levels of the mind of the distracting and dissipating thoughts with which it is usually occupied, and enable it to become single or one-pointed in our search for God.

We shall come to this in more detail later. But first we may turn to the difficulties which some people experience when we speak of this way of prayer. They will ask if this is not vain repetition and will remind us that Jesus warned against that. We must note, if we agree to make the Authorised Version translation the basis of our reply, that Jesus warned against *vain* repetition and not against repetition as such. Vain repetition – compare with vain argument or vain anything else – is repetition which does not do the work it is intended to do. If our intention in using repetitive prayer is that through it the Holy Spirit may deepen our communion with God, then the repetition is vain or not according to whether that end is defeated or realized.

Recently I preached a sermon in the parish church on the saying of the rosary. About a dozen people were truly grateful; the others were, I think, a bit surprised, and it may be that some reacted unfavourably. Unfortunately, I had not started with the parable of the wayside cow! Afterwards, someone said to me in the vestry that if he had said a prayer once he could not see the point of saying it over and over again. I tried to explain that on starting out for church that morning I had begun by putting each foot forward once and then I repeated the process over and over again; that this made quite a lot of sense to me because after I had done it two hundred and fifty times I was five hundred steps closer to the altar of God, and after four hundred repetitions I was right there. I think he thought that was cheating, but it is a very good illustration of what happens when one uses repetitive prayer. Every saying of the prayer with such attention or devotion as may be given us – and we are not to worry when the attention strays (as it is bound to do) so long as the intention remains – takes us one step nearer to the heart of God. If we look closely at the analogy of walking to church, there is in fact no repetition; that is to say not if we regard the *total* situation, for then a step taken outside my house becomes different from a step taken outside the church. It is just the same in the saying of the prayer. We shall come to the rosary later, but meanwhile let it be said that everyone who uses it knows that the saying of the fifth decade, by which time we are more drawn in to the heart of God, is a different experience from the saying of the first. Every bead, like successive hammer blows, takes us nearer to the place where we would be. Remember always that the function of the words is to establish the heart in prayer. Once they have done that, they have done all they were intended to do. The real prayer is not the words (though the words help to create it and maintain it) but what is going on beneath the words. The words are a framework rather as its banks are a framework for a river. It is the river which really matters, though it needs the banks to keep its flow constant and deep.

Another question people will ask is this: is not the prayer you describe simply mechanical? Certainly there is a mechanical element within it, but that is not the main part nor is it the most important. As I type out the pages of this book I am engaged in something obviously mechanical, but much the most important part of what is being done is not at the level of the fingers but of the mind and will. It is the same with the rosary. Just as the tapping of the keys is at this moment important to the progress of this book, so the passing of the fingers through the beads of the rosary is important to the development of the prayer. But it is the heart and mind and will which make it so. I imagine that it would be easy enough nowadays to make a robot which would perform the rosary day and night. This might be to make prayer merely mechanical, and when our objector questions that, it will be time to listen again.[3]

It is in fact the mechanical support which the rosary brings to prayer which makes it of such help. For, first, it breaks the time up into small elements, enabling them to be dealt with one by one. Secondly, the pressure of the fingers on each successive bead is an aid to keeping the mind from wandering. Thirdly, the breaking up into five decades (I shall explain this later) relieves the monotony of the exercise. Fourthly, the beads which remain to be worked are an encouragement to continue to the end. And, finally, the audible repetition of the words helps to gather the attention into what is being done. Yet none of this would be of the least importance if the heart and mind and will were not directing the operation and finding their own movement within it. The mind, however, is not now working discursively as in our ordinary occupations. The frequent repetition of the same words works towards turning the mind away from discursive meditation, making it one-pointed and setting it free to pray at a level below that of the conscious mind.

Let us now turn our attention to the saying of the rosary. We have already said that it has a long and honourable tradition in the Roman Catholic Church. A Catholic paper which describes it as 'merely a monotonous and boring relic of past ages when few could read' reveals a pathetic lack of awareness of the importance it may have for many people today. And these are by no means only the simple and uneducated; nor yet are they simply Catholic Christians. That massive and perceptive philosopher and theologian, Baron von Hügel, regularly used the rosary; John Wesley used it and his rosary is in the possession of The Leys School in Cambridge; and the distinguished Anglican theologian, Dr Austin Farrer, found it in his later life an invaluable help in his prayers.

The illustration here shows a rosary; it consists of a circle of beads to which at one point is attached a short strand of five beads ending with a crucifix (it may be sometimes a cross). This strand is known as the pendant and it is here that the saying of the rosary is begun. We begin with the Apostles' Creed, with the forefinger and thumb on the cross or crucifix, and then, taking the first bead in the same way, the Our Father is said. A Hail Mary is said on each of the next three beads (which are spaced on their own and signify faith, hope and love) and a Gloria ('Glory be to the Father . . .') on the fifth. Then with the thumb and forefinger at the place where the three strands are held together, the Our Father may be said to start the first decade. A Hail Mary is said on each of the ten beads which follow and a Gloria on the spaced bead at the end. The same bead serves to start off the next decade with an Our Father and the same pattern is repeated until the fifth and last decade is completed, followed by a Gloria. The devotion may be closed in any way we choose. The collect for the Annunciation makes an appropriate ending. In this way the saying of the rosary may be expected to take twelve or fifteen minutes.

The Hail Mary, which is repeated fifty-

three times (five decades plus three for the pendant) in a complete round, consists of the words:

Hail Mary, full of grace, the Lord is with thee, blessed art thou among women and blessed is the fruit of thy womb, Jesus. Holy Mary, mother of God, pray for us sinners now and at the hour of our death.

The other two rosaries shown are ring rosaries, the top one made of metal and the other of wood. These are designed to slip on to the forefinger and the beads are worked by the pressure of the thumb. It may be more convenient at times to use them otherwise. This type allows for a single decade of the Hail Mary preceded by an Our Father and followed by a Gloria when the decade is completed.

Associated with the rosary are fifteen 'mysteries', five known as joyful, five as sorrowful, and five as glorious. With each of these is linked an event in the life of Jesus or his mother and there are Scripture passages to help us recall them to mind. This is helpful to some but to others it will be a distraction. That would certainly be so for me, so rather than attempt to write about what I have no experience of, I will ask readers who may be interested to refer to books which deal with them. Neville Ward's book *Five for Sorrow, Ten for Joy*[4] makes an excellent study. Neville Ward is a Methodist minister who believes that Methodists would do well to make a place for the rosary in their way of prayer.

I have come to use the rosary regularly and I would like to explain why I find it helpful.

First, it brings one right into the centre of the Communion of Saints. Mary stands, not alone, but at the head of the company of the redeemed, and in asking for her prayers I express my desire for the prayers of the whole company of heaven, that great cloud of witnesses whose work it is to encourage us in the arena of life.

Secondly, it is homely and simple. I am making a simple, though profound, profession of faith and I am asking for the prayers of others and being given a chance to depend on them. In that way I am learning to become indebted to others. Pride makes us want to be doing things for other people and thus we put them into our debt. We are the givers and they are the humble receivers, and, provided we have already learnt to be givers and still are when the occasion calls for it, a time comes when it is often more healthy for us to be receivers instead. It would have been easy

for Peter to have washed the feet of Jesus, yet it was the one
thing necessary that he should himself submit.

Thirdly, in saying the rosary I have a sense of solidarity with
others, for I know that millions throughout the world will be doing
the same thing each day.

But there is, too, one further point, which may be well worth
noting. The rosary may be found to provide an excellent basis for
intercessory prayer. Each bead, or each decade, or however we
choose to make it, can be offered for some person or cause.
Instead of making our own prayer for the person concerned, we
ask another to pray for us both. There is great advantage in this.
I expect we have all noticed how easy it is to become patronizing
or condescending in the matter of intercessory prayer. It is, no
doubt, very nice of me to say that I will pray for you, but perhaps
you will find yourself asking whether I think you need my prayer
that much, and whether it would not have been happier if I had
asked you to pray for me. One way of overcoming this problem
of condescension is to pray for another with thanksgiving, as Paul
so often insists. If we can say to another that every day we thank
God for them as we remember them in our prayers, we put
ourselves into their debt and not them into ours. We are indebted
to them because they give us cause for thankfulness. But sometimes that would be unreal, so another way is to lay ourselves
alongside the other person and ask a third to pray for us: 'Pray
for us sinners now and at the hour of our death.' Whoever we
are, we are fallen people standing equally in the need of the grace
of God, and this rosary prayer captures that thought exactly. If
we feel ill at ease invoking Mary, as some brought up in a non-
Catholic tradition may do, another well-known prayer may come
to our aid in laying us alongside another as we pray: 'O Saviour
of the world, who by thy cross and precious blood hast redeemed
us, save us and help us, we humbly beseech thee, O Lord.'

The rosary may be adapted to a great variety of usage. The
Jesus Prayer may be used on each of the ten beads with perhaps
a Gloria on the spaced bead. Some may take a verse from the
Psalms or elsewhere, or prefer to use words which have arisen
spontaneously from the heart. But it should be noted that too
great a variation is not advisable. It takes a long time and years
rather than months for a pattern to become firmly rooted in the
heart. If anyone on reading these pages decides to begin using
the rosary, it would make a good Lenten exercise, because it

would perhaps take them from Ash Wednesday until Easter with
a complete round each morning and evening before it became a
sufficiently deep reality in their lives for them to want not to lose
it.

Perhaps this is the moment in which something may be said of
intercession. Broadly speaking, I would divide it into two categor-
ies. There is the type of intercession whereby one prays directly
to God for some cause we have at heart: that, for example, John
may find a good wife or that Jane may find employment. Some
find it difficult to pray on these lines not knowing whether,
perhaps, God may be wanting John to be a celibate or Jane to be
working simply within the family. This type of prayer is, however,
'saved' by the if-it-be-thy-will clause which sceptics will see as an
inbuilt face-saving device and Christians will see, not as safeguard-
ing, but as governing, their prayer.

In the other category we put everything into the hands of God,
not presuming to imply the best outcome. We do this, for
example, in the Hail Mary of which we have just spoken, where,
putting our whole confidence in God, we trust him to work as he
sees best. The first category is illustrated in Scripture by the story
of the nobleman's son.[5] There is a sense of urgency in such prayer:
'Sir, come down ere my child die.' The second is illustrated in the
story of Martha and Mary sending a message to Jesus: 'He whom
thou lovest is sick.'[6] The matter is quietly placed in God's hands
and the outcome is left to him.

The trouble with this second type of prayer is that it can all too
easily become an extremely shallow replica of the real thing.
Someone buttonholes us after church, perhaps, and relates the
distressing symptoms of some relative or friend.'Ah well,' we say
after a few minutes, easily and glibly, seeing this as the best chance
of getting back to breakfast and the household chores, 'it's all in
God's hands.' Disengaging ourselves we go on our way and as
likely as not give to the matter no further thought or prayer.

Far, far superior to that is the nobleman's urgent cry: 'Sir, you
must come, you cannot fail me, my child's life depends on you.'
I recall in a parish situation how a woman came to me, begging
me to pray for her husband who was suffering from cancer. She
told me that the doctors had given him about a year to live.
'Father, you will pray, won't you, you really will?' I promised to
do so and after a few days she was back with the same request

and again and again over the weeks and months. Then, after about nine months, she returned, this time calm and collected, and she said: 'It's all right, everything is all right, he's in God's hands, may his will be done.' Now that was the real prayer. She had passed through the agony, and it is, I think, only after we have, in one situation or another, passed through the agony, that we may be fully entitled to use this second way of prayer without serious risk of self-deception. Perhaps we ought never to pray that God's will be done in regard to another person's trial until there is a good chance that we would be able to pray in the same way in regard to a similar trial of our own. These thoughts are intended to be challenging rather than to be given too literal an application, for I believe that if we persist in praying that God's will be done, as we are bidden to do in the Lord's Prayer, and pray as sincerely as we can, we shall be taken into new riches in Christ, whereby the prayer itself takes on a new depth of meaning. Father O'Brien, formerly superior-general of the Society of St John the Evangelist, writes as follows to a sister who has consulted him:

> In regard to intercession it has always seemed to me quite a simple matter for you. Your intercessions follow your mental prayer, and the inability to use considerations and a multiplicity of acts follows you into your intercessory efforts. As you say, the needs are innumerable and bewildering. For some their way of prayer would be to enumerate these before God and plead with him – this is genuine intercession – but you cannot do this and there is no need for you to attempt it. It is as though a beloved daughter came into the presence of her father with tears, and stood before him in silence knowing that he knew why she was there and fully sympathized with her unspoken request. Words would help nothing.

The full words of the Jesus Prayer are: 'Lord Jesus Christ, Son of the living God, have mercy upon me, a sinner.' The prayer may be shortened, if desired, and sometimes simply the word Jesus is held in the stillness of the heart. At that stage the prayer may or may not be framed by the lips. The beginner ought to be warned against excessive zeal at the start. While too fragmentary use of this prayer is of very little value, excessive use may open up the unconscious to a degree beyond which the emerging forces can be contained. Ten or fifteen minutes (of whatever form of

devotion may be chosen) for two periods each day makes a suitable beginner's guide, and growth can take place from there.

There is another prayer word which many like to use. This is
the word *Maranatha*, used by St Paul in the concluding verses of
his First Letter to the Corinthians. It is an Aramaic word which
may have been in frequent use in the early Church and it means
'Come, Lord, come'. Some people find it a help to use a word
such as this from another language because they are not then
tempted to use their imagination on images which the word may
conjure up (which are none), as in the case of a word in everyday
use. However, it is good that the word should have Christian
associations and for myself I find it best to use the English just
occasionally. The word should be used so that every syllable
receives equal stress: *Mah-rah-nah-thah*; and the '*ahs*' can be
lengthened as seems best. This has become for some a very
powerful mantra (as the Eastern word is for repetitive prayer)
and lends itself easily for silent use. It also easily combines with
the breathing, which some find a help, and in a person well
accustomed to it can answer deeply from within. Explanation here
or elsewhere is best given by those whose experience is deepest
and the interested reader is referred to books on the subject by
the Benedictine monk John Main.[7]

Another form of prayer which many may find helpful to carry
in the heart is that which from time to time may find expression
in the words 'thanks be to God'. I recall being greatly helped
when a priest said to me, 'Try thanking God for everything'. It
was of course St Paul's advice, and coming from one who had
met and passed through the challenge of almost superhuman
suffering it must reach us with great authority. It may perhaps be
asked what right we lesser people have to commend it. But at
least we can make an attempt to thank God for all the little
aggravations and frustrations as they meet us, and there is nothing
hypocritical about this because contrary events do give us the
opportunity of exercising patience, which for the Christian is a
gift to be prized more than wealth or honour. The saints have
often said that their enemies are in reality their greatest friends
and no doubt it is partly this sort of consideration which influenced
them. Archbishop Temple used to say that if we prayed for
patience God would answer our prayer by giving us opportunities
in which to exercise it, and that could never be unless we met
with contrary events from time to time. If we lived in that spirit

we can never, for example, and it is only one among many, experience an unprofitable sermon. If the sermon is good we may be edified by it, and if it is bad we may exercise patience and be edified yet more by that. Whichever way it is, we give thanks. We are truly on a winning wicket here!

Yet it needs to be said that, generally speaking, we must give thanks to God in the power of faith and not of sight. I recall my disappointment more than fifty years ago when I was turned down for my first post, one which I had set my heart on; yet a month later I was offered another which made me thankful that the first had been refused me. I ought of course to have thanked God in the power of faith from the moment the first disappointing news had arrived, but instead I missed a whole month before saying it in the power of sight, a poor substitute, and much time was lost in between. Again and again we shall find that the habit of thanking God throws us back upon faith and there can be no surer foundation on which our life can be built. Even so, it is often only possible to give thanks to God with the will, and the feelings may take some while to catch up. The habit also enables us to give particular effect to St Paul's great saying that all things work together for good to them that love God.

There are many forms which may express and develop the prayer of the heart. In time of temptation it may be the simple words, 'Jesus, hear and save'; in distraction it may be these words from *The Cloud of Unknowing*, 'Him I covet, him I seek, and him alone'; in doubt it can be, 'O send out thy light and thy truth that they may lead me'; in anxiety it might be, 'grace, mercy and peace from God the Father and our Lord Jesus Christ'; in disturbance, 'Be still and know that I am God'. And so we might go on. But it is best to have one main prayer and to stay with that for a good long time, and not to leap about as a bird hopping from branch to branch which will simply defeat all that we want God to do.

Let us now suppose that we have chosen our form of prayer, which perhaps we say on the rosary or perhaps we do not. Now let us ask what we are to do when distractions make their way in, as they surely will. The answer here is that we are to continue with the words of the prayer, allowing the heart as far as possible to be gently enfolded in them as before and, without attending to the distraction, we are to allow it simply to be there and to find its way out when it will. The distraction can even be of help in encouraging us to give renewed attention to our prayer. So far as the will is concerned, the distraction is handed over to God; but so far as the feelings are concerned, it is still with us and it must be suffered until it is taken from us. We treat it and bear it, in fact, just as we treat and bear some mild physical pain. One writer on the Jesus Prayer bids us allow the distraction to be absorbed in the name of Jesus, and this gives a vivid and powerful image. We are not to feel guilty about the distraction. We did not seek it and now that it is here we do not follow it or develop it. We simply continue with our prayer.

Finally, a word which may be of help in the use of every form of repetitive prayer. At the beginning the attention may be largely on our speaking the words. Later we shall find it is moving towards listening to them being said. This is a proper development. Instead of our saying the prayer it seems rather as if the prayer is saying us. We must let the prayer do its own work and resist the temptation to try to make something happen. Basically, prayer is waiting upon God until he delivers us. Repetitive prayer expresses our willingness for God to take hold of us when he will. We need to proceed firmly, but gently, awaiting God's time and not our own.

Notes

1 The chapter title is based on words of St Anthony of Egypt (*c.* 251–356): 'I psalmed down the devil'.

2 *Letters from Baron von Hügel to a Niece* by Gwendolen Greene. Dent 1928 (pp. 23–4).

3 I have deliberately written 'might' because, although the whole idea seems grotesque, it is in principle no different from the long-established custom of the lighting of candles by the faithful, by which means the devotion of many is sincerely expressed. I must say that I hope it will never come!

4 *Five for Sorrow, Ten for Joy* by Neville Ward. Epworth Press 1971.

5 John 4:46–53 (AV).

6 John 11:3 (AV).

7 See the following books by John Main, osb: *Moment of Christ* (Darton Longman and Todd 1984); *Word into Silence* (Darton Longman and Todd 1980); *Christian Meditation: Prayer in the Tradition of John Cassian* (1975). The last is a 24-page pamphlet available from the Grail Centre, 1066 London Road, Alvaston, Derby.

Sitting Still in the House

The chapter heading is taken from a verse in St John's Gospel.[1] Jesus had come to Bethany after the death of Lazarus and we read that whereas Martha went out to meet him Mary 'sat still in the house'. The translation is from the Authorised Version of the Bible and it has to be said that although it is attractive for our purpose it is not quite accurate. The Revised Version of 1884 better expresses the meaning of the Greek with 'Mary still sat in the house', meaning not necessarily that she was motionless, though I suspect she was, but that she had been sitting before and still continued to do so.

I find it interesting to note that three modern translations render the passage as 'Mary stayed at home'. This translation, offered perhaps as a concession to modern readers, avoids the clear meaning of the Greek which is also reinforced by two subsequent references to Mary later rising up. In the Living New Testament there is almost a conspiracy of deception, for both these references are mistranslated and there is here no mention of her 'rising quickly' or of others seeing that 'she rose up hastily'. At all costs, it seems, the idea must be conveyed that Mary was engaged in something 'useful'. Modern readers should not get the idea that Mary might have been occupied in anything so unproductive as sitting in the house. We might even be tempted to do the same. What a right old mess the Church would be in then! Yet what we of the Western Church need to take to heart more than anything else is the importance of learning to 'sit' in the house. 'Silence', writes Mother Mary Clare, 'is the doorway into the need of the world.' 'All the troubles of life come upon us', writes Pascal, 'because we refuse to sit quietly for a while in our rooms.'

I remember calling at a Christian home in India to pay my respects on the death of a parishioner. When I reached the house it was to find the corpse laid out in an open coffin in the sitting-room surrounded by chairs which were mostly occupied. We sat there quietly in prayer. It seemed a much more dignified way of honouring the dead than happens in the West, where we meet the bereaved at a moment when silence is their deepest need, searching for suitable words as though the dead needed our eulogy rather than our prayers. I have no doubt that the scene in Bethany was not very different from that in India, except, of course, that at the time of which we are speaking, the body of Lazarus was already in the tomb.

Lazarus had been dead four days when Jesus arrived. His body would probably have been taken to the tomb on the first or second day, depending on the climate, and the removal of the corpse would have marked the end of the strict period of mourning when no food might be prepared in the house. As soon as the body was removed, all the furniture would have been turned round to face the walls and low stools brought into the room on which the mourners would sit. The days of weeping lasted for three days after death and then on this, the fourth day, began what was known as the period of silent grief. Mary and her friends would have been sitting in silent prayer together, and it was not until she received, through Martha, the call of Jesus that she broke her silence and rose to meet him.

How is it that we may learn the prayer which springs from the stillness which Mary knew? In the first place, is it a way of prayer which God intends for us all? There is much evidence to suggest that many are being called in this manner today, and I think that most committed Christians may expect it to be sooner or later the way which God has in store for them. If, therefore, we have not already received the call, we may wait expectantly for it. Our way, perhaps, has been for many years that of meditating upon a passage from the Bible which has then become the basis for a brief self-examination and the forming of a resolution. This is often referred to as discursive meditation and it has been the foundation of the early prayer life of many. Yet it commonly happens that there comes a time when it is no longer satisfying. Even more than that it becomes almost impossible, and this is not because we are less committed or less eager for God than before. On the contrary we want him now more than ever and we find a growing longing for him and him alone. Our desire now is to put our Bible reading on one side and simply to be still in the presence of God. This does not mean that there are not to be times when we return to the Bible and other Christian books to learn more of our faith in that way. It is in fact probable that at other times we shall want to do this more than before. It simply means that the way of discursive meditation belongs no longer to what we would want to call our real prayer life. This now seems to lie beyond. Before, we were turning from the things of the world to attend to the things of God. Now, we are turning from the things of God to attend to God himself. This is an advance to be welcomed. It is the difference between wanting to know all about a friend, which may be a very good thing to do; and wanting to know our friend and experience his or her love and friendship, which is better still.

What, now, is the way forward? It may well be that we are not yet ready to put away a book completely. We are like children learning to walk who need a rail to hold on to now and again. There is a well-recognized way of prayer which lies between discursive meditation and that of silent contemplative prayer. It may be called affective prayer or the prayer of aspiration. There are many books which may help us here, but it may be that none are better than the Book of Psalms and that is within easy reach of us all. Those familiar with the Book of Common Prayer may well prefer that version. Others may like to use the Alternative Service Book (ASB) or one of the many good translations available.

Using this method we turn to a Psalm: perhaps it is Psalm 62. We read a verse, or it may be a part of a verse, and then pause, allowing the words to dissolve within us as a sweet may dissolve in the mouth. With the ASB before me I read: 'My soul waits in silence before God.' I pause. I do not try to think discursively on the words. I do not attempt to analyse or develop them. I allow them to rest on my mind, letting the mind take them gently to the heart. I allow them to fade away and return if that happens to be so or to remain as long as they will and then disappear. My pause may be quite a brief one, say ten or fifteen seconds, or it may last for a minute or even several minutes. When the flavour of the sentence is exhausted I take the book again and read on: 'For from him comes my salvation.' Another pause, and then: 'He only is my rock and my salvation' . . . 'my strong tower' . . . 'so that I shall never be moved.'

Then, as so often happens in the Psalms, a few verses become quite unsuitable for our purpose. It is best to discover this before we begin, as it makes a distraction at the time. Here we have to move on to verse 5, and we can continue as before to verse 8, by which time there may have been about fifteen pauses lasting perhaps, on average, a minute each. That is enough food for one session. However, what is important is not the amount we read but the time we spend, and on some days just two or three sentences may be sufficient to fill the whole time. There are many Psalms which might be used in this way, but it is worth noting that the same may be chosen again and again and it may be rewarding to do so. Many books other than the Bible may, too, be profitably used. For example, one might use the quotation which concludes chapter 1 of this book.

The stage beyond, that of complete silence without the help of a book, is not very different from what we have described. Instead of having a number of aspirations we usually have just one which acts as a focal point for the mind so that when it wanders, as it surely will, it can be led back to this point again and again. Some like to have a sentence such as 'Be still, and know that I am God' or 'Abide in me and I in you'. The Bible, and especially the Psalms, will yield a harvest of such sayings. However, we may choose something shorter, perhaps just a single word such as God or Jesus.

There are days, and it may be particularly at first, when the time passes easily and quickly, but more often it may seem like an uphill road needing patience and perseverance to the end. In this way of prayer the fourteenth-century *Cloud of Unknowing* is a book which has been a guide and encouragement to many. I do not want to speak much of it here, as I have written several books in which it is prominent and repetition would be inevitable.[2] However, it may be useful to introduce the reader to it – though many will already know it – and it can then be explored through one of the several editions available. In chapter 3 we read:

> Lift up your heart to God with a humble stirring of love, and mean God himself and not what you get from him.
> Be on your guard lest you think of anything but God himself. Let nothing occupy your mind and will but only God.
> Do everything you can to forget all God's creatures and their activities, so that nothing holds your mind or desire whether it be in general or particular.
> Let them be, and pay no attention to them.

Thoughts will inevitably come into the mind, but *The Cloud* at this point says that we are simply to let them be, it being assumed that we have not wanted them nor encouraged them. If we let them alone, trying as far as we can to attend only to God – and in this we may be assisted by the sentence or word we are using – they will have no power over us, and, as we shall see in the next chapter, they may have an important function to fulfil. Our task is to look to God and not to attend to them, which does not of course mean that we shall not be aware of them. To use a favourite *Cloud* image, which comes much later in the book, we try to look over their shoulder to God who is beyond.

This work may demand a great deal of us, and in the words of *The Cloud*: 'When you first begin you will find only darkness and, as it were, a cloud of unknowing.' The writer continues, in chapter 5:

> You cannot feel what it is except that you feel in your will a naked reaching out to God.
>
> This cloud and this darkness, no matter what you do, is between you and your God. It prevents you from seeing him clearly with your mind and from experiencing the sweetness of his love in your heart.

We are not to be discouraged by this. It is fatal to think of giving up just because things don't seem to be going well. The temptation is often likely to be that we are doing nothing at all and that we are just wasting our time. If, however, we were to change our occupation and really do nothing – or even do some simple task – it would seem so absurdly undemanding that it ought to persuade us that we must have been fully occupied before.

The Cloud goes on to insist that we shall persevere. It continues:

> Prepare yourself to wait in this darkness as long as you may, ever calling after him whom you love.
>
> If ever you shall feel him or see him – as far as is possible here below – it must always be in this cloud and this darkness.
>
> If you will but work on earnestly as I bid you, I believe that in his mercy you will win through.

With these encouraging words we shall leave *The Cloud*. Readers not familiar with it may like to pursue it on their own.

An important part of our prayer is the posture. It is important not for its own sake but because it helps the mind and will to do what they have set out to do. This is obvious enough in other activities such as going to sleep or writing a letter, but it is often overlooked in the realm of prayer. When you go to sleep you take up the posture which will most easily enable sleep to take over and when we go to prayer it is the same, only it is God whom we hope will come to us. This, if you like, is our part of the bargain, doing what we can to enable God to reach us. It may sound rather foolish talking like that, but God does expect us to do what we can. The servants at Cana were not able to do anything in the way of wine-making, but they were expected to fill the water-pots and we are told that they filled them to the brim. Those who watched by the grave of Lazarus could not bring him back to life, but they were told to remove the stone which sealed him in the tomb. Nothing that we do can determine the way in which God comes to us, but we can show him with our bodies that we want him and do our best to prepare ourselves for him. When and how the bridegroom comes is his business and not ours. Let us at least be ready with oil in our lamps.

The basic factor about posture is the straight back. The back is to be held in a firm but easy tension making allowance, of course, for the natural curvature of the spine. The neck will be erect, the head straight, the chin in a middle position, that is to say neither held in nor pushed out, and the mouth lightly closed.

Many from the East and some from the West favour the lotus posture, sitting either on a mat or on a low Zen cushion. Readers who want to know more of this should find a teacher or consult a specialist book. I am assuming that most who read here will want to sit on an upright chair or bench, or to kneel upright, or to kneel and sit back on their heels or on a cushion placed over the calves. Some may like to use a prayer stool placed across their calves, when kneeling, which they then sit on. It may be that sometimes we shall want to stand. Whichever way it is, the straight back is common to all.

It will be best to begin with a conscious act of relaxation. Take up whatever position you have chosen and speak gently to your body to encourage it to relax. Start with the brow and temples and move on to the muscles of the face and those around the eyes and see that the jaw muscles are relaxed. Observe that the shoulders are down and pay special attention to the arms and hands. The hands can rest palms downwards on the top of the thighs or can be folded in the lap with palms upwards. A good relaxation will make the arms and hands feel warmer. It is important to speak gently to the body; otherwise it will not respond. It is best to see relaxation as something which is allowed to happen, and ourselves as simply doing what lies in our limited power to help it happen. After one or two minutes look mentally towards the heart, and when you find the mind going off on some journey of its own and become conscious of it (which may not be at once), bring it back gently with the word or sentence you are using.

I myself often find it helpful to use two short sentences: 'Let go' and 'Let God'. They are a reminder that God's action is all important and that our part is to enable him to act as far as we can. These sentences also assist relaxation of the whole person, mind and body, and it is the holding of tensions which often prevents us from being open to God. We know well enough how something similar is true in human relationships. A social gathering is often stiff and formal at first and it is only after the mood has relaxed that we may begin really to meet one another. You can keep returning to these sentences from time to time, and sometimes you can add a third: 'Let be'. 'Let go'; 'Let be'; and 'Let God'. The middle sentence refers to any distractions of which we may be aware, and it is a reminder that we are simply to suffer them and allow them to be, until, ourselves attending to God, they go of their own accord.

Many who find silent prayer difficult (and who does not?) may be helped if they come to realize the importance of bodily stillness. Thus if we are using, as suggested earlier, the words 'Be still, and know that I am God' we should let them apply to our bodies as well as our minds. Our bodies are, in fact, much more under our immediate control than our minds, and the mind will tend to fall into line with what is happening at the level of the body. By stillness of body is meant absolute stillness, so that if a small object were placed on the head it would remain there, or so that the fingers on the thigh or in the lap do not move by a fraction of an inch from the chosen position. Moving the body occasionally, however, does not matter provided it is deliberately willed and attended to; it is the unconscious fidgeting which is prejudicial to what we are attempting to do. Even to be absolutely still, in the sense described, for a single minute can be a severe test for those unaccustomed to it; though, too, a discovery when its fruits are realized. It can be worth while spending an entire prayer time in offering the sacrifice of bodily stillness. There is, however, one point to watch: as the back straightens out, as it surely will, the position should be adjusted to accommodate this movement.

There is, too, another position for prayer and it is a perfectly respectable one. It has, in fact, the authority of St Ignatius Loyola (and, too, of Father Augustine Baker of 'Holy Wisdom') as one of several postures. In Eastern tradition it commonly follows a period in the upright posture. It is to lie flat on one's back on the floor or some other firm surface. A single pillow or cushion may help, but see that it is well drawn down to the shoulders (not under them) so that the neck as well as the head is supported. Feet should be a little apart and arms should be slightly out from the side. Palms can be facing downwards or upwards as preferred.

Do not be afraid of this posture in prayer. I like to think of it as the posture of receiving. That does not mean that we do not receive in other positions, but we may be here more conscious of what we are receiving than of what we are giving. Perhaps that is very good for us. To say that is not in reality to contradict the saying of Jesus that it is more blessed to give than to receive. Receiving may itself be the most costly way of giving, the sort of giving which calls for the surrender of a little bit of our pride and is in no way flattering to our self-esteem.

Here in this position we may, if we so like to consider it, receive the prayers which others make for us. We often ask how we may learn to pray better; seldom do we inquire how we may better receive the prayers of others. It is surely part of the completeness of prayer that we should learn to do so. Lie on your back and tell God that you are there to absorb all that he would give you. Let the tensions drop away one by one, for it is this which makes you receptive to the Spirit's gifts. 'Breathe on me, breath of God' – tell God you are wanting him to do just that. Allow yourself to be refreshed by what God would bring you, and when the thought crosses your mind that you are being plain lazy treat it with the disdain which it deserves. It often takes much persuasion before Christian people will use this posture for prayer; it seems such a little thing and threatens the activist image we have of ourselves. Yet it is a valuable alternative to the more widely used postures and it is likely that we shall value it increasingly as we grow older. 'Into your hands I commend my spirit.' God has, after all, ordained that for most of us the final commendation is to be made from the position of lying on our backs.

I have suggested two phrases which might be used. But we must find the one which best meets our need. 'Underneath are the everlasting arms' is another powerfully suggestive phrase and may often be right at such times. If that is our choice, then so often as we return to it we think of ourselves as sinking into God's arms which are bearing us up. We are to be careful not to fight thoughts which may come into the mind. We are to let them go even as they came without following them or getting involved in them. If we are new to the back posture we shall soon discover that it takes as much resolution to stay with it to the end as in the more common positions.

A word of warning needs to be given. Some people say that when they are feeling tired they will use this position and that when they are fresh they will use one of the others. If you use the back posture do not keep it for when you are tired. If you do you will almost certainly go to sleep, and although it is an admirable thing to go to sleep in the arms of God it is a different thing from what is being described here.

Earlier it was said that we should look mentally to the heart, and there is a long tradition of this in Christian prayer. 'Put your mind into your heart and stand in the presence of God all the day long' is the advice of one of the early desert fathers. Although it is best to start with the heart centre and perhaps to stay with it all our lives it is not the only point open to us. In the Zen tradition, for example, the centre is often found in the region of the belly at a point known as the tanden, about two inches below the navel. It is an imaginary point; there is nothing to see nor for a doctor to remove! If you find your prayer wanting to go down to that point don't be afraid of it. You will be conscious that, as you breathe out almost as far as you can go, exercising the lower part of the lungs which are too often starved of air, there will be a slight tension at the tanden point. You breathe out slowly – as it were with the brakes on – and this creates the tension of which we speak. When the breath is held out for a few seconds at the lowest point, that is to say with the lungs 'empty', we become still more aware of it. If it seems to you that you are taken to this point go with it and don't resist. It is well known that the belly marks one of the psychic centres of the body and perhaps Jesus was recognizing this when he said that out of the belly would flow rivers of living water; and it will be remembered that the evangelist comments that he was speaking of the Spirit.[3] It is true that the

Greek word *koilia* is translated differently in modern versions, and perhaps that does not much matter, but the Greek most naturally indicates the belly and I think that the Authorised Version has a real point in keeping to it. One interesting thing about holding this slight pressure at the tanden on the downward breath, and on the few seconds when the breath is held out, is that the thinking process is inhibited and this may help on a difficult day in preventing us from developing and following up distractions. It should be said that if you are taken to this point, all unneeded tensions above the navel are to be released. Instead, the tension is gathered in the tanden.

In case we are taken to this point in prayer we shall only be acting in correspondence with what nature often bids us do: the body has a way of knowing what is best for it in the building up of its vital energies. A person receiving a letter which he thinks contains bad news will probably open it with 'bated breath' and this brief holding of the breath produces the tension of which we are speaking. He needs special energies at such a moment and instinctively he finds them. If you thread a needle or read something with deep concentration you will find the same thing happening. It is the same with the artist as he prepares for a delicate stroke; or the marksman as he prepares to fire. The grunt of exertion breathed out every time a Wimbledon celebrity serves to an opponent is evidence of neither belligerence nor affectation but of the gathering of tanden strength at a moment when every ounce of energy is needed. Laughter produces considerable tanden tension, which must be one reason why it is so good for us. If, then, our prayer wants to go to this lower centre there may be good reason for it. I am saying no more than advising you to keep a certain flexibility and to remember that your body is a friend assisting you in your prayer and asking you to treat it with the respect it deserves.

Notes

1 John 11:20.
2 See the note at the end of the Preface. The quotations which follow are taken from *The Dart of Longing Love: Daily Readings with the Cloud of Unknowing*. Darton Longman and Todd 1983.
3 John 7:38–9.

7

My Fair Lady

It may often happen in silent prayer that we become suddenly aware that our mind has been engaged on some train of thought without our intending it or without even knowing that we were occupied in this way. Our task then is to bring the mind back gently to its centre, helped perhaps by a word or sentence held in the heart. We have experienced what is technically known as an involuntary distraction, that is to say a distraction in which the will plays no part. It is important to note that we are not to allow ourselves to be troubled by such distractions, for not only are they bound to arise but it is necessary that they should do so. It is through distractions arising spontaneously from the unconscious that we are brought into touch with our deeper selves. Martin Buber relates a story, in his *Tales of the Hasidim*, in which the disciples of a new Jewish teacher were worried about his teaching. They went, accordingly, to a neighbouring rabbi, renowned for his holiness, and they asked him how they might resolve their problem. 'Go back', said the rabbi, 'and ask your teacher what you are to do to prevent distracting thoughts intruding in the time of prayer. If he tells you how to prevent the intrusion of such thoughts you will know that he is not to be followed, because this advice would show that he had never understood the truth that distractions must occur again and again right up until the time of death.'

Distractions come from many sources some of which are due to outward events acting upon one or other of our senses. Those which come from visual objects we can deal with simply by the closing of our eyes, but the other senses do not allow for such an easy remedy. A neighbour's radio, the smell of cooking from the kitchen, or itching shoulders are examples in which three of our senses are involved. But there are, too, those which come from within, and it is likely that these may be much more troublesome. Outward stimuli, such as noise or smell, cease after a while but what is within us follows us wherever we go. We are attached, sometimes obsessively, to forces within, and these attachments have to be loosened.

The story is told of two Zen monks, both of them young men, who were returning to their monastery which lay some miles back from the bank of a river they needed to cross. When they reached the ford they saw a beautiful young woman who feared to make the crossing lest the waters were too strong for her. Young Zen monks are not supposed to have dealings with young women but the elder one, seeing her plight, put her on to his shoulders and carried her to the opposite bank. After he had set her down, the two monks continued on their journey. They walked in silence for a mile or two, after which the younger one exclaimed, 'Whatever made you carry that young woman across the river?' 'Good gracious,' came the reply, 'are you still carrying her?'

No doubt we would all like to resemble the elder monk, possessing that degree of detachment which enables us to pass from one occupation to the next, giving our full attention to each successive task in hand, without being disturbed by the memories of the earlier work. He laid his burden down on the river bank, not simply in a physical sense, but in such a way that he might continue his journey without harking back to what had gone before. We are, for the most part, like the younger man carrying in some degree our burdens and anxieties from one occupation to another. Such observations, however, interpret the story only at a superficial level. At a deeper level we carry with us a great deal of the junk of the past, not just of yesterday nor of last week, but all the way back to the earliest years, and we carry it not as an external burden, in which case we could put it down when we liked, but as something well mixed up within us: fears, griefs, greeds, memories of all kinds, which though normally latent may rise up at any moment to disturb and sometimes to torment. In the silence of prayer it is likely that these ghosts, normally residing below the threshold of consciousness, will rise into the conscious mind, impressing themselves upon the imagination. The very first thing to get clear is that when this happens, provided it has not been sought, nor is voluntarily developed, it is to be welcomed, for the memories are there that they may be healed.

William Johnston, in his book *The Mirror Mind*, expresses with great force the thought we are developing:

As the contemplative life develops, it simplifies. Words become fewer; silence predominates; inner words rise up from the deeper areas of the psyche and from the centre of the soul. And at this time other things also surface from the unconscious, things that need to be healed – suppressed fears, anguish, all kinds of hurts. Now one continues to sit in the presence of God in a situation that is paradoxically filled with joy and filled with anguish. Here there is a strange mixture of peace and pain.

And this is the beginning of the dark night. Now I must not push these hurts into the unconscious; I must not bury them, I must not flee from the ghosts and the dragons and the wild beasts that leer and smirk and grimace. It does not help to run away either to watch television or to play golf or to throw myself into frenetic work. However laudable these activities in themselves, now is not the time for them. Now is the time to sit quietly with God even when the whole inner life becomes desperately painful, even when all hell seems to break loose inside me. I must let it all surface. I must face the devil. But (and this is important) while I *watch* all this material as it comes up, I must not *analyse* it or *get involved* with it. I must not be seduced by the wild figures from the unconscious; I must not let them engage me in treacherous dialogue. No, no, I must remain with God in the cloud of unknowing, simply watching them and watching myself with compassion.

Painful, you will say. Yes, very painful . . . But the suffering and the pain need not disturb me. It has to be so. There seems to be a direct relationship between healing and suffering. In order to be healed one must suffer . . . And through this painful process the memory is being healed. The hurts and pains that have been lurking in the psyche from early childhood, from the moment of birth, from the time in the womb, from the moment of conception – all of these are floating to the surface and are being healed by the love of the indwelling Spirit in whose presence one quietly sits.[1]

Here, then, is the transformation which is taking place in prayer as distractions rise up and threaten to take hold of us. We note that we are to allow them to be there, recognizing them but not voluntarily attending to them; meanwhile, the disturbance they cause may continue and has to be suffered as part of the total offering of our prayer. Our prayers are not likely to be the neatly-

rounded-off exercises we would wish to see and we are to resist
the temptation to try to make them so. Our grime and our sweat,
provided there is love in it, is more likely to be for the glory of
God and the healing of his people, and it is worth remembering
that sometimes as we pray. Ultimately the two stand together. In
the words of Irenaeus: 'The glory of God is a living man, and the
life of man consists in beholding God.'

If this be the work of prayer we may well ask who can afford
to neglect it? This 'sitting in the house' may indeed be the most
important thing we ever learn to do. If the giving of our lives to
one another is important, yet the quality of the life we have to
give is more important still. I recall reading of a priest who came
to Carl Jung, worn out by work and near to breakdown, seeking
the advice he so desperately needed. Jung told him that he should
work only eight hours a day instead of his usual fourteen and that
when his work was done he should go into his study and sit alone
until it was time for him to retire to bed. After two weeks he was
to return and report his progress. He came back as advised but
his condition was no better. Jung questioned him and found that
he had spent his time reading or listening to music. He explained
to him that he wanted him simply to sit quietly by himself.
Becoming alarmed, the priest replied fearfully: 'Do you mean all
by myself? I know of no worse company.' Jung's classic reply was:
'Yet that is the company you inflict on your parish for fourteen
hours a day.'

In the previous chapter the point was made that some people
might be finding the tanden point a natural centre in prayer. It is
quite possible for this to happen on some days and not on others.
We are presumably being taken to the point to which we need to
go. I want now to speak briefly to those who may sometimes
experience prayer centred at this lower point.

We said that thinking was inhibited if the breath was pressed
down on the tanden. In his important book *Zen Training*[2] Katsuki
Sekida imagines his pupil practising Zen meditation looking at a
hill or a building or a picture. He writes:

This inhibition can be sustained so long as the breath is stopped
or almost stopped. It is true that your eyes are reflecting the
images of outside objects, but 'perception' does not occur. No
thinking of the hill, no idea of the building or the picture, no

mental process concerning things inside or outside your mind will appear. Your eyes will simply reflect the image of outside objects as a mirror reflects them.

If readers are dubious they might try this simple experiment. Ask a friend to give you two numbers to add together. Suppose you are given 43 and 29. You will probably add them in a few seconds without difficulty. Now hold your breath hard down on the tanden and ask your friend to give you two more numbers of similar difficulty. I think you will not be able to add them until you have released the pressure.

What we are saying clearly has relevance in dealing with distractions in prayer. I have written elsewhere of a Zen image in which you see yourself on a bridge looking over the parapet into a river which is flowing beneath. On the river are empty boats and these stand for the distractions flowing along with the stream of consciousness in prayer. Zen says that you are to watch the boats as they go under the bridge but you are to resist the temptation to jump on board. My point at this moment is that it is the pressing down upon the tanden which in fact makes it impossible for us to board the boats and travel in them through the treacherous waters to which they may take us.

What is now being said could have a close bearing on many situations. But especially it might be helpful to any who have acute fears amounting perhaps to phobias. Many of us have something of this sort – sometimes absurdly ridiculous in their seeming irrationality – tucked away in our skeleton cupboard. Tanden practice does not mean that the fear (or it may be some other emotion such as jealousy or anger) will not emerge, but that when it presents itself so that a little healing can be done on it, then it can be watched without being developed or followed. I am writing on this not because I want to introduce something 'way out' to the Christian reader but because it may be that he or she can be helped as I have been. If the well from which you now drink yields waters which quench your thirst, then by all means leave this on one side. Yet Jesus is reported as having said that out of the belly shall flow rivers of living water, and I do not think the metaphor is simply an idle one.

One of the Zen masters speaks of the healing power of what we have described both towards the one who practises it and to those around, saying that a mentally sick person in another room would receive benefit. The saying is similar to one from *The Cloud of Unknowing* where the author claims that his 'work' helps 'wonderfully' all mankind, more than any of us can ever be aware. He adds that 'even the very souls in purgatory find their pains eased by virtue of it'. It is important that we should take this thought into our prayers for we never operate as isolated units, except in outward appearance, but always as men and women within the communion of saints. The one who prays becomes through grace a centre of spiritual energy – the energy of love – and as a stone dropped in a pond sends ripples to each bank, so the healing power of love radiates from the still centre within to all mankind. This I affirm simply as an article of faith, supported, no doubt, in the knowledge that many others have done the same. The atmosphere which certain churches and shrines and other places carry with them is its own witness to this truth. Our work thus becomes most truly a work of intercession offered, it may be, specifically for this cause or that, or simply in the most general sense for all people according to their needs.

Robert Hugh Benson's story of a nun kneeling in silent adoration before the Blessed Sacrament, linked as by an unseen light – 'the atmosphere was charged with energy' – with all mankind in its needs, is already well known to many.[3] It comes to my mind just now as we are in the middle of a Billy Graham campaign in Norwich; and at St Julian's church we have a chain of prayer through the day in which the faithful come to sit for an hour at a time before the Blessed Sacrament which is exposed upon the altar. It is our way, and we believe it to be a right and effective way, of invoking God's blessing upon the campaign; and, as prayer is always a reciprocal event, it is true, too, that through the silence the *essence* of the evangelist's message will become more firmly rooted in the hearts of those who watch in prayer.

Perhaps we ought to have gone to the meetings as well. Some did. I am always rather torn at such meetings. A part of me makes me feel that when the call comes I should go forward. Which of us has ever made the true turning to Christ? And another part tells me to remain in my seat. And so, perhaps, it was only to be expected that as I sat there in the church one of my favourite stories should come back to me. Rabbi Feivish of Zarach went to Rabbi Mendel to spend the Sabbath with him. On taking his farewell he wept and said: 'My brother, I am seventy-four years old and still I have not truly turned to God.' Weeping, Rabbi Mendel replied: 'My brother, that troubles me too.' So they knelt together and blessed one another with the blessing that each might be able to make the true turning.[4] The joy in heaven must have been complete. I, too, am seventy-four. Coincidence! Let it stand as a sign that we are to encourage one another.

But we must return to our nun. Teilhard de Chardin retells Benson's story. To the ordinary observer, there is nothing to be seen in that chapel except a silent figure before the Blessed Sacrament. But to the visionary who discovers her, the unseen world is revealed. De Chardin continues:

> All at once he [the visionary] sees the whole world bound up and moving and organizing itself around this out-of-the-way spot, in tune with the intensity and inflection of that puny praying figure. The convent chapel has become the axis about which the earth revolves. The contemplative sensitized and animated all things because she believed; and her faith was operative because her very pure soul placed her near to God. This piece of fiction is an admirable parable. If we could see the light invisible as we could see the clouds or lightning or rays of the sun, a pure soul would seem as active in this world by virtue of its sheer purity, as the snowy summits whose impassible peaks breathe in continually for us the roving power of the high atmosphere.

In writing as I have done in this chapter I am not wanting to press one way over another but simply to introduce the reader to a practice which may on occasions mark the way forward. While the prayer of the heart is the Christian norm we are not necessarily to be tied to it but to be open always to the beckoning of the Spirit. Whichever way it may be, the 'work' will, in the words of *The Cloud*, 'so suffuse body and soul . . . that all good people [observing those who practise it] will be glad and happy to have them in their company, and would know that in God's grace they were strengthened and cheered by their presence'. Such a person, the author adds, will 'be at ease with all who would speak to him – "saints" and "sinners" alike – without being drawn into sin himself, and all this to the astonishment of those who see him, and at the same time drawing them through grace to the work in which he is being formed'.

Probably most of us know people for whom these words are true. They may yet become so for ourselves.

'Therefore,' continues the writer, 'get this gift – all who by grace may have it.'[5]

Notes

1 William Johnston, SJ, *The Mirror Mind*. Collins 1981.
2 Katsuki Sekida, *Zen Training*. New York and Tokyo, Weatherill 1948. It may be interesting to note that the 'Sin! sin! sin! Out! out! out!' of *The Cloud of Unknowing* (ch. 39–40) makes use of this inhibition (unconsciously no doubt). You cannot say 'Out!' vigorously without considerable tanden pressure, whether said outwardly as *The Cloud* allows or inwardly as it commends.
3 R. H. Benson, *The Light Invisible*. Hutchinson, n. d.
4 See *Tales of the Hasidim* ('The Later Masters', p. 137) by Martin Buber. Schocken Books, New York, 1948.
5 The quotations draw on ch. 54 of *The Cloud of Unknowing* and are taken from *The Dart of Longing Love*.

Appendix

The following may be useful for those who want to learn more about tanden practice.

First you should know something about the breathing. If full lung capacity is 60 decilitres, normal breathing is between 28 and 23 (at 18 breaths a minute) and 'empty' lungs is 12. You can never go below 12, and in tanden breathing you go down to a point just above 12, leaving enough breath in the lungs so that you could just say a few words if you had to do so. However, we shall call the point 12.

Tanden breathing is from 28 to 12. It is the exercising of the lower part of the lungs which is important. The outward breath is made slowly so that you feel a pressure at the tanden point 2 inches below the navel. At first the outward breath may take about 4 seconds.

For those interested in physical details it may be said that when you thus breathe out 'with the brakes on', the diaphragm and the belly are working in opposition. In normal breathing they work together like two horses in harness. In breathing out 'with the brakes on', the belly is trying to squeeze air out of the lungs and the diaphragm is resisting this. Hence the tension felt at the tanden.

When you reach the point 12, pause, holding your breath out. You will feel the pressure at the tanden. The belly is trying to hold the air out, the diaphragm is wanting to let it in. Hence the tension. After several seconds, release the belly. Your clothing should be loose enough to enable this to happen easily. As the belly expands, the diaphragm is enabled to fall and the lower part of the lungs will open as a pair of bellows, creating a vacuum allowing the air to enter with a smooth flow. Don't 'sniff' the air. Let it come at its own pace.

Timing: Perhaps at first 4:3:2, meaning 4 seconds on the outward breath; 3 seconds on the pause at the end; 2 seconds on the inward breath. This gives about 7 breaths a minute. Later you will find 3 breaths a minute to be about right. But be content with 4 or 5 or 6. You can vary the first two figures of the 4:3:2 as you please but keep the 2 about constant and let the outward breath be not less than 3 seconds. At a later stage 4:6:2 would make a good rhythm. Don't hesitate to take 'recovery' breaths if you need them, that is to say several normal breaths between 28 and 23 in between the tanden breaths. After a long pause at 12 let the inward breath go up to whatever level it wants and allow it to take 3 or 4 seconds.

Important: Feel the tension at the tanden (except on the inward breath) and release all unnecessary tensions above the navel. You will feel a tendency to tense in the face and elsewhere. Release the tensions. *Zen Training*, referred to in the notes to chapter 7, will give you full instructions.

Another valuable book is *Hara* by K. von Dürckheim (Allen and Unwin). *Hara* means belly. At the end of this book there are more than a hundred sayings by the Zen master Okada. Some of them are:

Sit quite still, breathe gently, giving out long breaths, the strength in the lower belly.

Gather your strength in one point only – in the lower belly.

In your head is no tanden. Do not put strength in your head.

Always, even when climbing a precipice, one should exhale very slowly, at the same time pressing strength into the tanden. Let us repeat – to strengthen *hara*, long, slow out-breathing. As if emptying a pump one must press his breath down into the belly. Most people lack this training in everyday life. So they know nothing about gathering strength in the belly.

Do not try to free yourself from all thoughts. Simply be watchful and keep strength in the belly.

What a pale face! If you practise yet look pale, and you don't begin to like a dish you disliked before, your work has been useless. Take unto yourself real learning and then you will look happy.

'Sitting' in a room next to that of a mentally disturbed person will produce a change, a transformation in that person.

Mrs X has given up her diamond ring. But what, after all, is a ring? If she did not cling to her life she could be happy. 'Sitting' means to give up one's 'I'.

A cypress increases its rings even as a very old tree. One should grow indeed until the moment of death.

From getting-up time until bedtime you must be awake (on the jump). Keep your posture in *hara*, come what may, and you will be alert in the right way.

The following passage is quoted from *The Three Pillars of Zen* by Roshi Philip Kapleau (Rider 1980):

Hara literally denotes the stomach and the functions of digestion, absorption and elimination connected with it. But it has parallel psychic and spiritual significance. According to Hindu and Buddhist yogic systems, there are a number of psychic centers in the body through which vital cosmic force or energy flows. Of the two such centers embraced within the *hara*, one is associated with the solar plexus, whose system of nerves governs the digestive processes and organs of elimination. *Hara* is thus a wellspring of vital psychic energies . . . the Zen novice is instructed to focus his mind constantly at the bottom of his *hara* (specifically, between the navel and the pelvis) and to radiate all mental and bodily activities from that region. With the body–mind's equilibrium centered in the *hara*, gradually a seat of consciousness, a focus of vital energy, is established there which influences the entire organism . . . an enhanced vitality and new sense of freedom are experienced throughout the body and mind, which are felt more and more to be a unity.